Your
Individual
Divinity

Existing in Parallel Realities

Your
Individual
Divinity

Existing in Parallel Realities

Liane Rich

The information contained in this book is not intended as a substitute for professional advice. Neither the publisher nor the author is engaged in rendering professional advice to the reader. The intent of the author is only to offer information of a general nature to assist you in your quest for emotional and spiritual well-being. In the event you use any of the information in this book for yourself, the author and the publisher assume no responsibility for your actions.

Loving Light Books
Copyright © 2015 Liane Rich

ISBN 13: 978-1-878480-32-3
ISBN 10: 1-878480-32-4

Loving Light Books
www.lovinglightbooks.com
Also Available at:
Amazon - www.amazon.com
Barnes & Noble - www.barnesandnoble.com

For Jack and his beloved Donna…
who loved Butterflies.

Higher Vibrating Streams of Energy

Lower Vibrating Streams of Energy

Parallel Realities

All realities are made up of vibrating energy. You are a multi-dimensional Being existing in more than one reality at any given time.

You may shift "up" to a higher version of you by focusing on a higher vibration.

High vibrational feelings are: Love, Gratitude, Happiness, Joy, Positive Thoughts, Acceptance and Kindness.

To use another analogy - say you have a game. Each level reached within the game carries a reward. It's not that you deserve or don't deserve the reward. The reward or gift is always there on that particular level and you have simply accessed that level.

"Hold on to the idea of perfect divine order. Do not be afraid to see behind the illusion to the perfection of creation...."

Preface

*W*hen you raise yourself to the level where the highest vibration realities exist you are going into a parallel reality; a reality that is already alive! The goal is to enter it and stay in it.

How? You stay in the highest vibration, or version of yourself and you are magnetically drawn to that parallel reality. You live there also - simultaneously - you just haven't focused on that reality as you have been busy focusing on your current reality.

It's not a future but a now! All parallel realities are here and now and they exist just as your current reality exists.

You may shift "up" to a higher version of you by focusing on a higher vibration. Certain "feelings" give you a "lift up" to the next vibration. These feelings are the ones I just listed (see previous page).

Once you raise yourself to a higher vibration you are magnetically drawn into the next higher vibrational stream of reality. You live where you choose to live by your choice of feelings. Low vibratory feelings draw you "into" a low vibrating stream of energy or a low vibrating parallel reality.

Gratitude is the most powerful of feelings simply

because you have less confusion around what gratitude is. It is almost impossible to be feeling thankful and be unhappy at the same moment!

Love is very confusing for all of you, simply because many equate love with sexual feelings and emotional feelings and attachments of all kind. Even addictions are sometimes seen as love.

Joy and happiness are not as complicated, however, with joy and happiness you can sometimes wish for things to happen to others that may bring you joy out of revenge.

With the energy of gratitude you may be grateful for someone else's pain but it is much less common. Normally you are thankful for things that turn out the way you want them to. If you can be thankful or grateful for everything you see in life, you will be unable to feel unhappy and this will be a huge "lift up" to your vibration.

Every time you add a little thankfulness, you add a little height to the level from which you operate, or the level from which you draw your creations to you.

You see, everything is already created! Everything that could possibly be imagined is already "alive" in the field of potentiality or the God force. Nothing that exists is wrong or bad or right or good. Everything, absolutely everything is simply energy in movement. Move your energy in the direction you choose. You may climb "up" the stairs or "down" the stairs depending on which level of the mansion you wish to experience. It's all just energy and you are simply on a tour of the mansion. You come and go often, and this is not your first, nor your last time to visit. Where would you like to go?

Note from Liane

For those of you who are new to God's books and curious to know more about the source of this information, I have published a small book titled, *For the Love of God - An Introduction to God.* This small book will give you a great deal of insight into this voice that speaks to me and writes through me.

For the Love of God – An Introduction to God also appears as the Introduction to our book titled, *The Book of Love.* Either book will give you greater insight into this voice and the source of this information.

In the back of this book you will find a brief description of my first encounter with the God voice as well as a full list of book titles.

I am told that repetition is used as a teaching tool in these books. God uses repetition freely and says that's the fastest way to get through our judgmental, conscious mind to the subconscious.

I hope you enjoy the insights presented here and that they may help you to have a happier, healthier and more peaceful life.

In loving light, *Liane*

Introduction

*Y*ou are at the beginning days of your rise up out of the denser or slower energy streams. You have been living in these slower forming energies for some time now and you are beginning to wake up, and in doing so you will begin to rise "up." This is what all the fuss is about when you hear talk about ascension. Ascension is a process of rising up and becoming aware of one's own divinity. Not only do you become aware of your true identity, you also become aware of this multi-dimensional world that you have been living in.

Your world is made up of energy on many levels. You have your high energy/high vibration currents and you have your low energy/low vibration currents. Most of you spend your time in the lower vibrations; however, many of you have caught on to how the higher vibrations may be accessed. This is no mistake. Many, at this time, have been learning how to access the higher vibrations in an effort to manifest a more pleasurable reality.

The trick to manifesting a more pleasurable reality is to stay in more pleasurable thoughts and feelings. This is true if you wish to affect your own personal reality, and also will affect the collective consciousness of your world.

So, if you choose to raise your vibration, you might do

so through your thoughts and your beliefs and your feelings. This is not the only way; however, it is probably the easiest way for most of you at this time. You are easily influenced and easily motivated by wealth and good health and things (material things) that bring you joy. The most important thing for you as a sentient being is that you rise up. The reasons for doing so do not matter. What does matter is that you finally begin to access the higher realms of vibration, and that you finally begin to see how powerfully divine you truly are.

This book is titled *Your Individual Divinity* as that is what we will be discussing throughout this text.

It's All Just Imagination...
God's Imagination

*E*ach individual spirit, soul, piece of God, gets to choose what to see. If you choose to see a comedy, you get to laugh a lot. If you choose to see a drama, you get to be serious. If you choose to see struggling, fighting and chaos you get to see struggling, fighting and chaos.

You choose the movie you wish to see and you become not just one of the characters, you become all of the characters in your movie. It's all imagination and individual pieces of God creating as God. It's all part of God's imagination and it's part of God. There is nothing but God and God is a giant dream. This is a dream that is taking place on a cellular level within the dream that is taking place on a global and universal level.

All life is a dream and all life is happening right now. No past, no future. There is only this dream and it is being imagined differently by many, many parts of God.

Remember - God is all inclusive. Nothing is left out of God and nothing exists but God. That includes you and it includes the guy who just shot his neighbor. It's all a dream that is taking place right inside of God.

God is vast indeed and you are simply a piece of God

that is focusing on this particular reality or dream. You are an individual expression of God. You are an individual divinity who lives within the whole of God. You are just a small part of all that makes up God simply because you are focusing only on this tiny, tiny dream within the imagination of the grandest dream of all. God dreams big and God contains all possibilities for any visible creation to be focused on.

You get it from God. You get your dream from within God because you *live* in God. You then become part of your dream in the same way you might rent a movie and then jump right in to play all the characters. You may select, or use, any movie you wish. All categories already exist within God. You need not worry that you chose an incorrect movie. Movies are always available to you and you get to return to select another one any time you wish. You simply turn off your current movie (dream) and view a new one.

*Y*ou are not yet fully aware of your true nature. You are divine! You are part of God and you do not allow for this to be possible. Once you begin to allow for your own divinity, you will be on the road to discovering how and why you are here.

Most of you do not believe that you exist beyond this human you who is sitting (or standing) reading this book. You believe you are a human who is struggling to survive on earth and I want you to know that you are not meant to struggle. You are meant to live a divinely beautiful life full of love and grace. To live a beautiful life you require a change in the direction you are going. You have been headed into a non-trusting way of living, and it is time to turn this around and to create a world and a life filled with *trust!* No longer will you fend off your fears and try to convince yourself that life is dangerous. Life is *not* dangerous, and you are simply so connected to and addicted to fear, and drama, and chaos, and struggle that you return again and again to these energy frequencies.

There is a new and better way and this is what we will be discussing throughout this book. You will find that although you are attached, and connected to, and addicted to fear, mistrust, and struggle, you will be able to turn this around in time and move to the higher frequency realities that contain great love and peace.

Once you turn around and move out of the lower frequencies, you will be able to disconnect with those energies and move forward to the higher vibrational frequencies. Remember - everything in life and beyond life is energy. You move towards the energy you are drawn to. If you are drawn to drama in life you may be full of drama from past experience. This could be from past life or from this life. Each individual is part of God experiencing as God. This simply means that you, your soul, is from God and part of God. Your soul is not a tiny piece of you. Your soul is the entire energy that makes you up. You are actually more space or emptiness than you are matter. You are actually more God energy than you are matter.

So, why don't you feel this God part of you and why don't you act like this part of you? You have not been taught how to tune in to the God *in* you. You have not been taught to accept the God in you. You are taught how human you are, and how mistake prone you are, and how evil and depraved you can be. No one took the time to teach you about your divine, trusting, loving nature. You are hiding the best part of you. You fear retribution and so you do not claim your divinity. Your divinity has been lost to you for so long that you *feel* far from divine.

This is the time to reconnect with your own divine self and to know how beautiful you truly are. This is the time to allow your divinity to shine. This is the time to move in the direction of waking up to the fact that, due to your divine creative nature, you have the ability to turn around and move in a whole new direction. This new direction requires a shift in energy. You are capable of shifting and moving energy. The energy that makes you up is constantly moving and changing. We are now going to focus on points of energy that we will then be attracted or drawn toward. In the same way that you might focus on a point of destination you can focus on a point of energy within an energy wave.

You might think of these waves as levels or as parallel waves one above the other. Your goal is to attract or *draw yourself into* one of the higher vibrational waves of energy. This allows you to surf or flow on a higher frequency vibration, which in turn allows you to feel *lighter* and happier. The goal here is to move you from the denser energies to the much lighter energies which were listed at the front of this book. So, if you wish to enter the lighter energies and become attracted to them instead of the lower energies, where you now reside, you may begin by focusing on those higher energies. This will literally *draw you* towards those higher energies that you are focusing on.

The reason these energies are called higher is simply because they vibrate at a much higher frequency. If you continue to vibrate at a very low frequency you can sometimes stop vibrating altogether, as you may lose momentum. With the higher/lighter frequencies you tend to *continue* on forever!

❧

*Y*ou are not the only living entity who has had an

identity crisis. Most of those who walk the earth are in a state of confusion as to who they are and how they exist.

Most of you believe that you came from God but some of you do not. Some of you believe that you came from a species of aliens and some believe they evolved out of the ethers. Regardless of your beliefs regarding your beginnings you are here now and you are, for the most part, confused and uninformed regarding your true nature. So, if you are from God, you are part of God. If you are from aliens you are part alien; and if you are from the ethers you are part of the ethers. It is all true and you are literally part of absolutely everything that exists. Yes! I am saying that aliens exist as well as much more that you, at this point in your existence, know nothing of.

So, if you come from the ethers, who created them and where did they come from? Who created time and space and how does it continue to exist? Most of what your scientists observe is a reflection of a giant God force. I call it God force; you may call it universe or force field or field of possibilities. All of you see what you see depending on where you stand; not on where you stand in reality, but where you stand inside your own self. The inside of you is the most important and most ignored part of you.

Say you have a telescope and you wish to look through it to view the stars. Wouldn't you say, or think, that the most valuable asset you own for viewing stars is your telescope? You, my friend, are this most valuable telescope. You cannot view stars without it. You may look up at the stars with the naked eye, but you see only a tiny speck compared to the fullness you receive from looking at the night sky through a telescope.

If your greatest joy and your greatest desire is to look at stars, wouldn't you consider your telescope to be most valuable? With this telescope you are allowed to see into space in a whole new and wonderful way. So, let's say you decided to take your telescope on vacation with you, and you end up having such a good time on vacation that you forget to use your telescope, and you forget about the stars and you simply enjoy your vacation? And you dance and you sing and you even meet someone special and you fall in love.

What becomes of your most valuable possession, your telescope? Nothing! Absolutely nothing. It is still sitting here waiting for you to return from your vacation. Your telescope is the part of you that you use to "observe." It is the part of you that you use to watch the show of life. Your telescope can literally transport you (your feelings) to great heights of ecstasy. You observe and you see spectacular views and you are awestruck. Do not lose this part of you. You have become so immersed in judgment and fear that you often forget to simply "observe" what is going on around you.

Now, I realize that it is difficult for you to observe when you are bombarded in your news with pictures of war and violence. I also realize that it is most difficult to let go of judgment when you are so lost in fear of death and fear of pain. If you can set aside your fears and begin to simply *observe without judgment,* everything will "shift" for you. In observing reality you literally change reality.

Most of you are unaware of your ability to shape your lives by *allowing* everything to simply "be." When you allow reality to be, you change the dynamics that make up reality. When you allow reality to "be," you stop pushing at reality and it will stop pushing at you. When you push at reality and say, "this is awful, this must change," you literally put out a signal that fills the ethers with "this is awful and must change." This signal permeates everything, and lifts you or lowers you (depending on the denseness of the energy involved) to the parallel reality where the judgment of "this is awful and must change" exists.

Yes! This reality already exists as all realities are alive within the field of potentiality that you live within. You live within the God force or the ethers that contain "All That Is." You move in and out of various waves of energy that are all alive and well within this field. Your strong desire that "this is awful and must change" draws you into a parallel wave, or reality, where "awful" exist. Eventually your vision will be so full of "awful" that you will be drawn to an even denser wave of reality.

Now, if you view your current reality and you can find some "good" in place of "awful," what energy frequency do you suppose you will be drawn to then? Yes! You can literally choose where to go by how you think or translate what you are viewing. Observation is good. Simply observe it and *allow* it to be. Observe life and allow it to unfold. If you are being chased by a lion, run like hell but try not to judge this reality as "awful." Why? Simply because you are energy and you live in a field of energy and energy moves and is magnetic in nature. You get to choose where you wish to go in life. You may go up or you may stay where you are, or you may choose to go lower - no judgment if you do. Energy moves and flows and sometimes energy sticks to you and sometimes you stick to it. Choose your reality and you will begin to move in that direction.

Note: I wasn't sure of the definition of ethers so looked it up in my old (1936) Webster's Collegiate Dictionary and found this – *Physics:* A medium postulated in the undulatory theory of light as permeating all space, and as transmitting transverse waves.

Liane

❦

*T*he most interesting part of being human is your ability to co-create. Many of you desire to be more than what you are. Some desire to be less important and some desire to be more important. It has become increasingly popular to be more important and to have notoriety. Notoriety can bring attention and fame and sometimes it can bring wealth with the fame. The most important part of your journey on earth is the development of your consciousness and your awareness. The more aware you can be of your inner workings, the greater your chance of rising up in vibration to a higher frequency.

When you raise yourself to the higher frequencies, you actually allow yourself to enter a new reality. Each reality is based on vibrations or wave frequencies. Each wave frequency matches its inhabitants. It is virtually impossible to live or exist in a wave, or reality, that vibrates lower or higher than you (as a human) vibrate. This affords you (the human) to access realities that match your frequency.

So, how many parallel realities are there? They are uncountable! They are so vast that they are infinite in nature.

Absolutely *everything* is already alive and created, and exists within this field of potentiality and possibility that *you* exist within. You draw yourself into each reality by allowing yourself to experience those thoughts and emotions that match the vibration of that particular reality.

I'm sure you have at some time heard a coach tell his team to "stay focused and don't get discouraged." This is an excellent way to get yourself up out of the denser feelings of "this is awful and I can't stand this." When you can tweak a feeling, or thought, to match a little bit higher vibration, you literally move yourself into a little bit higher reality wave or frequency. It doesn't take much to lift you just a bit. Sometimes it is a matter of just standing still, or being still and not getting all riled-up.

So, what do we do about your emotions in these instances? We simply allow them to rise up within the body and release. They are energy waves, or waves of emotion within you, and they will pass right through you if they are not acted on. So, choose your actions wisely and try to act on the higher waves of emotion. Higher waves of emotion would be an urge to hug someone or to complement them. Lower waves of emotion would be an urge to punch someone or to argue with them, or to put them down in some way. Remember - when you put them down you go down with them. It does not matter who it is or what the situation is. When you are sending out the denser energy of anger, you are the one who is being affected. You are using a dense energy vibration to create your reality when you could pass on the denser energies and act on the higher energies.

Like attracts like in the field of possibilities. It's all there just waiting for you gods to use at your desire. You may create whatever you wish for yourself. You are not a victim of the world you see. You are literally drawing yourself into a movie that matches your vibration. You may choose to see your current movie as awful and terrible, or you may choose to calm down and *focus on* or "believe" that something good is right around the corner. When the waves of an ocean are banging at the sides of your ship, you want to stay calm and not cuss out the God who sent the waves, as you will be cussing out you and putting you down into an even lower frequency vibration.

Do not be afraid of this information. It is not being written to frighten you, it is being written to guide you and help you. You are going lower than you wish to go and it is time for you to rise up. You may rise up in an instant. Simply breathe in and breathe out and float with the energy. Do not fear, do not worry, simply trust! Trust that you are going to float "up" once you stop putting yourself down by putting the world down. Let yourself accept each situation and you will be on the rise.

I know that you think you have all the answers and you want to save the world, but there is an easier way. Move "up" to a new way of thinking and you will move into a higher vibration with a whole new movie. Everything is being projected out of you onto the screen of life. I am trying, with this information, to get you into a much higher parallel reality. You get to choose. If you enjoy your current reality, you may stay. If not, you may wish to continue reading and learn more about how to access the higher dimensions. It is all up to you as you have free will, and free will allows you to go to any reality you choose. You are part of God and God does no wrong. Higher or lower - it does not matter. It's just that you seem to be ready to move up to a higher level and create and receive all the higher vibrational frequencies such as love, joy, peace and happiness.

Do not sell yourself short. You are divine in nature. Your divinity allows you to be absolutely anything you choose to be. Divine reality is where you will eventually all end up. You are an individual divinity and you are part of absolutely everything. Why not express love in place of fear and mistrust? Why not express and feel *trust* more often than mistrust? Trust will lead you in the direction you wish to go. Trust says to the field of all possibilities, "I know this will work out for the best." What kind of a message are you sending out when you send, "I know this will work out for the best?" If you are energy and magnetic (like attracts like) don't you think you will be drawn into a matching frequency wave or reality where "everything works out for the best?"

Let it go! Let all worry and fear and mistrust go. You need not do anything physically. You need not focus on anything mentally. You simply let go of your need to judge and condemn and put down. Rise above by allowing everything to simply "be." Do not judge it or bring it down in any way. Whenever you bring it down you bring *you* down to a lower vibrating reality.

Do you want to live in the higher realms and experience higher thoughts and feelings? Let go of your *hold* on the lower frequencies!

*W*henever you begin to delve into the workings of your behavior, you become a little uncomfortable. You do not like to look at your own behavior, as you are so judgmental that you constantly judge your own self as not good enough. This allows you to put yourself down even lower on the vibration scale. So, in order to allow yourself to raise your vibration it is a good idea to let go of judgment.

By judgment I mean any feelings of inadequacy that you have concerning your own behavior. If you believe you behave in disgusting ways, I would suggest that you either *accept* your ways or change your ways. It does not matter what you decide since we are not discussing morality here, we are simply discussing energy. You are energy, I am energy, absolutely everything is energy. It does not matter what you do so much as it matters *how you feel* about what you do.

You have always been taught to abide by rules and regulations, and often this causes you to "feel" guilty when, or if, you break the rules you are taught to live by. Most of you carry some degree of guilt energy and some of you carry huge amounts of guilt energy. The most important thing to remember about guilt is that it sends you very low on the vibration scale. Your frequency may drop considerably if you carry huge quantities of guilt energy. To assist you I highly suggest "forgiveness." Allow yourself to forgive and to love (accept) yourself just as you are. You do not require a facelift or a tummy tuck so much as you require self-forgiveness and acceptance.

Now, I know this idea is not exactly popular right now, but I would love to see all the children of earth begin to accept and love being exactly who they are this very

27

moment. Do not wait for a future when you look perfect. Allow yourself to be in love with life by allowing yourself to be in love with you. When you hold judgments such as, "I'm not good enough" or, "I'm not attractive enough," you are putting you *down* in a very big way. This energy put down will affect you a little each time you express it to yourself. You will slow your vibration by the tiniest bit and then tomorrow, when you express this judgment again, you will slow your vibration the tiniest bit again. And this goes on day in and day out until you simply stop vibrating. I would suggest that you change this type of behavior. You are slowing your own life vibration by judging you.

Then we have situations whereby you judge your neighbor and try to put your neighbor down. Who's energy do you think you are affecting in this situation? Your neighbor won't feel your feelings, you will. Your neighbor won't think your thoughts, you will. Who's energy level will drop in this situation? Not your neighbors....

So, if you wish to bring your energy "up," please begin to see the benefit in raising your level of vibration in order to ride, or live, in a higher vibration reality. You get to choose where you wish to live by how you "decide" to use your power. You are powerful by nature and I don't mean muscular power, I mean creative power. You have the ability to transform yourself by how you *perceive* absolutely everything. Do you want beauty in your life? Then I suggest you find a way to look for the beauty *in* you. You are your life. You are projecting your life out onto the viewing screen of reality, and it is being reflected right back to you. The ugliness that you see is all in your mind. It is in the way that you are translating what you see. Look at it differently and you will begin to see your projected images change. It is all coming from you and you have the power to see it differently, and by so doing you change the projected image that you are looking at.

Many of you have heard the saying that "life is a mirror reflecting back to you that which is in you." This is true. You are sending out an image that is being reflected back to you by putting you in the reality you have chosen. You are being put into a moving wave of energy that carries the exact vibration that you are sending out. You chose to go to this exact location, or parallel reality, by "feeling strongly" about something. When you feel strongly about something you begin to move in that direction. That direction is then the choice you have made. You now have chosen a movie, or a parallel reality, to live in for that moment in time.

Over time you may move into and out of other realities based on how you feel, think, believe and behave. God is never punishing or rewarding you. God is simply *allowing* you to be the creative energy beings that you are. You are divine and you do no wrong. You create! That's what you do. You have free will and you create. You are an individual divine spirit that is creative by nature. You are a particle of God and you do not yet see that you are. You have the divine ability to move into any dimension, or reality, that you choose. You simply do not realize that you have this talent and so you do not yet know how to use it for your best interest.

You will learn... it is as though you are learning to walk. First you must try to stand and keep from falling. Next you must put one foot in front of the other, and it helps if you hold on to something for support. Then, eventually, you will let go of your support and you will walk freely, and before you know it you will run. Right now you are learning to stand and keep your balance; and right now very few of you know what balance feels like. You go back and forth between self-disgust and self-acceptance. The more you can stay in self-acceptance the greater will be your ability to stay in balance. When in balance your energy is calm and peaceful and smooth. You vibrate at a very high, smooth frequency when you are in balance and out of the judgment put down.

Your frequency affects your life, and your balance affects your frequency. Stay in balance and in acceptance of you, and you will be drawn into a movie, or reality, that is in balance and showing acceptance of you.

⁂

*A*s you begin to see how you have the ability to access greater levels of reality, I wish you to remember that you are human and fallible. Often you think everything should be perfect without any fluctuation. When you are dealing with energy there will always be fluctuation. Energy moves in waves and energy flows within you as well as around you.

So, if you are looking for perfection you will only find it by *allowing* energy to be in movement. Once you realize that there are ups and downs, or ebb and flow, you will be more readily accepting "All That Is." "All That Is" does not begin and end. "All That Is" does not sit stagnate in perfect harmony. "All That Is" moves, and you must be *willing* to move *with*, and not fight against, the energy if you wish to attain flow and freedom of movement. Once you are flowing with the energy you will begin to see how pleasurable your existence can become.

Some of you are so afraid of change that you fight every little movement in a new direction. You are fighting with change and you do not trust change. Change is what energy creates when it moves. You live in a flexible field of possibilities. How can you not change and move when *you* are literally made up of energy?

So, as you learn to flow with your current reality you will open the possibility of an even better reality. There really is no better or worse since it's all energy; but since you live in a human body, I will use your terms of judgment for greater understanding. So, if you wish to move on "up" to a higher vibration reality, I would suggest that you *allow* life to occur without getting too defensive and riled-up about it. Once you are flowing in your current reality, you will begin to access the higher vibration realities simply because you will be vibrating faster by the act of *accepting*.

Acceptance is a very powerful tool and may be used in order to achieve your goal of rising up. Acceptance allows you to sit in a situation and calmly observe it in order to see how you will work *with* the energy of this particular situation. Throughout this book, and the others that I have channeled through Liane, acceptance is equated with *love*. Love is acceptance and acceptance is love. You embrace life by accepting life and you embrace another by your acceptance of them. We are not discussing romantic love or attraction here. We are discussing open acceptance which is basically *allowing everything to simply "be" what it is without judging*

31

it to death. Once you can reach a place of acceptance, you will be in a very good position to move on up.

So, as you learn to accept and embrace life just as it is, I wish you to allow for changes in your life. Change is always frightening for you and you like to hide in your current state. Change, however, is inevitable when one is made of energy. You are an energy being living in an energy field. How can you possibly not move and change? So, I see you are getting nervous with all this talk of change, so I will move on to other topics.

This time I will discuss your health. Most of you would welcome a little change in your health, and this would be a good time to introduce you to a whole new healthy way of living. This new healthy way of living includes a positive attitude. With a positive attitude you are happy and carefree. When you are carefree you are calm and peace loving. I wish you to stay peace loving and let go of your *need* to fight with everyone and everything. When you are peace loving you are calm, and you are not causing the energy field around you to fluctuate. When you are fighting and pushing at people and life, you are literally causing larger waves of energy to occur within the field of energy that you live in. You can calm the waves you live in by calming you. You create larger waves, or surges, in the field you live in by the choices you make. You affect energy and its movement in the same way that energy affects you.

If you find yourself in a big wave or surge of energy, your best course of action is to stay calm, accept the energy and allow it to move past you, and in some cases, when the energy is coming from within you, allow it to move *through* you. You are energy, you live *in* energy and everything around you is energy. Do not be afraid of acceptance. You have become so fearful that you sometimes fear what is very good for you. You have become so defensive that you push at energy constantly, and this will eventually wear you out and break down your health. So, stay healthy by going with the flow of energy until it comes to a good place for you to move in a new direction. It is like a ride on a wave, and you will be brought to a safe shore if you flow with it long enough, and observe the conditions of the water in order to guide yourself as you ride this big wave of energy.

Here is the good news about energy: "everything comes to an end by changing into something else." Energy changes and moves, so it will always be changing and moving. This is what you do. You change and you move into something else. You do not literally end. You never end. Just as energy never literally ends, it simply changes and moves on, you simply change and move on....

☙❧

*Y*ou may wish to continue to live as you have always lived and that is just fine. You may also decide to raise your vibration and that will allow you to feel even better about your life.

If you are unhappy with your life in any way whatsoever, you will be glad to know that you can reverse your unhappy feelings. When you decide to look at life in a new way, you literally give your life (and your world) new meaning. Say you have been unhappy in your role as parent or guardian. Once you begin to appreciate the role of parent or guardian that you have taken on, you will feel happier in that role. Appreciation is a powerful tool for you in your journey through life. Appreciate and accept all that you can. You may not appreciate someone's comments to you and you may not appreciate someone's attitude towards you, however, you may learn to appreciate the role that this individual plays in your life. This individual may be in your life to assist you in advancing on a spiritual level. Maybe this individual is you from another dimension and is simply showing you where (within you) you have energy blockages.

I realize that on earth you do not have the ability to *see* who you are and where you come from. This inhibits your ability to recognize other you's who are existing right alongside you. In my previous books, the *Loving Light Books* series, I explained for you how parallel you's might bump up against this particular you in this particular life. This is true and these parallel you's do have an influence on you from time to time. Now I am suggesting that you may have another you who is living in this current life, either near you or at a great distance from you.

These other you's are made up of your same soul energy that split off from you before entering this earth plane. These other you's may be family members or they may not be known to you. Sometimes you may dream of them, and sometimes you may have a sense or feeling that there is someone out there somewhere that is connected to you.

Think about it! If you all come from the same place and you are all made up of energy, is it not possible that this energy that makes you up is also in another human form? You are energy beings living in a body that *appears* to be solid matter, but is actually more energy than it is matter. You are more nothing then you are something. The space that makes you up is spirit energy. The space that fills you is spirit energy. You are energy and you think this energy is containable and it is not. You may appear in more than one place at a time and you may inhabit more than one body at a time.

Now, once you begin to understand how you, as a spirit, can be in more than one place at a time you will better understand your dreams. You like to travel and escape the body whenever possible and this is what is taking place at this time. You are all traveling out of body and experiencing in other realms and other dimensions, and you even visit one another at times when you sleep. You are energy and you go wherever you wish and you see whomever you wish.

So, why do I bring this up now? It is time to begin to understand who you are. You are so much more than you realize. You are in the infancy stage of your human development and you have so much to learn about being you. The first thing to learn is "stay focused on you!" You get sidetracked by focusing on the projected reality that is going on around you. You are bombarded with news and events that are going on around you, and I will tell you now that the way to self realization is to focus on the self. The self sends out the signals that draw you into a particular movie theater or parallel reality.

Remember, it's all here already created in this field of possibilities. You simply get *drawn in*, or some would say *sucked in,* to this or that reality by your own focus. So, focus on what you want. Do you want controversy or do you want a peaceful existence? Both movies are playing. Which do you *choose* to see today?

⚜

*Y*ou are about to enter a new way of thinking which will allow you to access a whole new view of life. This new way of thinking makes it possible for you to begin to see yourself and life in a new way.

You are not so sure you believe in the one and only God scenario, but it is the one you have been taught and most of you *accept* this scenario as truth. You, however, do not believe it is possible to be God or even part of God, as you have decided that you are the one who creates all your problems. You judge yourself as a sinner and you *know* that you cause problems for yourself and for others. You believe that you are not wanted, and you try your best to do things that will make you feel accepted by society. You are afraid that you are not good enough to be included and to be loved. This fear gives you an inferiority complex and it causes you to feel bad about yourself. Once you are feeling bad about yourself you begin to judge and to criticize life and everything in it!

You are judging and criticizing life because you feel fearful and you do not know how to come out of your fearful thoughts. You come out of your fearful thoughts by changing them or switching over to *acceptance.* You need not spend hours working on changing you if you can just learn to catch your thoughts before they build and blow up into something bigger. When you have a disturbing thought, or a revengeful thought, or even a sad thought, catch yourself before you expand that thought. Catch yourself and tell yourself that, "Everything will be okay." This simple act will allow you to keep your disturbing thought from taking you deeper into the denser energy of fear and mistrust.

As you continue to use this technique you will find that you are not only accepting life, you are creating a happier, more positive life for yourself. "What about the violence and the awfulness that is all around" - you shout! I will tell you now that *you* are deforming the energy and blowing it way out of proportion. You are then projecting this blown up version onto your viewing screen of life. Do people die and suffer in this world? Yes, they do. Is it awful and horrifying? That depends on how you see it. You have been drawing yourself into the awfulness of life for long enough. It is time to begin to focus on and to draw your self "up" into the higher, lighter energies. Some may call this a Pollyanna effect, however, it works!

So, as you consider giving up fear and *allowing* everything to "be," you will be allowing yourself to "be." You are the one who is picking on you. You are the one who is bullying you. You are the one who is putting *you* down, and now you *feel* so put down by life that you want to criticize and put life and everyone in it down. You are putting you down by putting them down. You draw yourself into a lower vibrating stream of energy, and this is where you live until you change your mind and move "up" to a higher vibrating stream of energy.

You may begin to see life and everything in it differently. You may begin to change your mind at any moment. What if earth was just a stage where spirit actors could come and play or act out roles? What if being in a human body is no different than being in a costume designed for this particular role in life? What if the actors have been "playing" in this material plane for infinity; and what if these roles were chosen ahead of time by the actors themselves? What if the better actors usually like the heavier roles that lead them, or allow them, to experience denser emotions? What if these spirit actors never really die, and only slip off stage to don yet another costume for the next role they have *chosen* to play? What if in the whole scheme of things there really is no death, and everyone and everything is simply energy that moves and changes into something else? What if you are in such a slow vibrating reality that you cannot see the whole, true picture? What if....?

*Y*ou are the one who decides where you will live. You may choose to live in a higher vibrating reality or you may drop down to a lower vibrating reality. This choice is made by you every minute of every day. This choice is not so much a feeling as it is a decision which is created by you and then enacted upon by you.

You need not judge your decisions. Judgment leads to suffering by punishment. Judgments often call for harsh reactions and anger. Allow yourself to choose to feel your feelings without getting too involved in them. You may ride your feelings or you may *allow* them to come up in you and pass right through you. When you allow them to pass through you, you avoid the ride. If you choose to ride the wave of feelings that come with judgment, you may find yourself being pushed down into deeper, harsher feelings. Feelings are created by your *reaction* to life. Sometimes you react negatively and at other times you react positively to life. You get to *choose* if you think life is good or if you think life is bad. This choice is usually based on several conditions. If you are afraid of certain outcomes, you will see those life situations as bad. If you are open to and accepting of certain outcomes, you will see those situations as good or okay for you.

So, you always decide! You always send "you" to good or to bad, or somewhere in between. Everything is a choice that you will make for yourself. If you have children or a spouse, you will try your best to send them in your direction. You do not wish to see them go off in a different direction simply because it frightens you. If you are happy and you see life as good and a gift, you will want to share this gift of goodness with those you love and care about. If you are afraid of the future "what ifs" that you are projecting for yourself, you will want to take those you love and care about into your fears with you, in an effort to protect them.

Here is the interesting part of being a creative being... you get to decide every moment of every day which reality you choose to live in. You may bring yourself "up" or you may put yourself "down." It is simply a choice. It is like living in an infinite mansion and exploring all the levels or floors of the mansion... no judgment please! You may go up or you may go down. You may hide in a corner or you may move all around and explore to your hearts content. You may create a love story for yourself or you may create a battlefield for yourself. You are an actor in a costume, and you may play or act out any role you choose. You may be the good guy, the bad guy, the thief, the hairdresser, the ballerina, the baker, the tycoon, the housewife, the warrior or the peacemaker. It is all simply a giant play that allows "you," the spirit you, to create.

So, what do you wish to create? Who do you feel like being today? You will find that the best way to treat you is to simply love you unconditionally until you can come out of judgment. Judgment holds you down and pushes you down and suffocates the spirit in you. You think harsh judgment crushes the dreams and aspirations of your loved ones and friends? You should see what judgment - self judgment - does to you. You do not enjoy being judged, so I am now asking you to stop!

You may determine the level of judgment that you carry by looking at how you see the world. If you are constantly criticizing and finding fault with your world and your life, you will do well to let go of some of this judgment. I would like you to spend one entire day lifting *yourself* up, by allowing yourself to see only the good in absolutely everything. If you judge eating meat, I wish you to think of all the starving who have been saved by eating meat. If you judge vegetarians, I wish you to think of all those vegetarians who have healed themselves by being vegetarian. Now, I do not expect you to rush out and convert from vegetarian to meat eater. I am simply saying, "Do not judge either one." If you are white do not judge blacks and if you are black do not judge whites. If you are married do not judge singles. If you are single do not judge marriage. If you are gay do not judge straights and if you are straight do not judge gays. If you are liberal do not judge conservatives and if you are conservative do not judge liberals. If you are religious do not judge atheists and if you are atheist do not judge religion.

You are judging you to death! You are running this energy of judgment, and in some cases hatred, through your body day in and day out. You judge your neighbors, you judge your parents, you judge your spouse, you judge your children, you judge your government, your relatives, strangers and even life. Give it a break please! Give you a break. Judgment suffocates your spirit. You are putting "you" down every time you run the energy of judgment *through* you. You are putting you down with the way *you* choose to see you. You see you as not good enough, not smart enough, not kind enough, not loving enough, not rich enough, not healthy enough, not protected enough, not safe enough, not bold enough, not fun enough, not flexible enough... just plain "not enough." And all of this "not enough" thinking and judgment puts you down into a "not enough" movie or reality.

You are creating "you" as you go. You are creating your reality as you go. Allow your reality to be okay and enough. Let go of judgment and *allow* everything and everyone to be okay and acceptable "as is." This will allow *you* to be okay and acceptable "as is." This will draw you further into a parallel reality that is okay and acceptable and judgment free. Lift you up to the next wave of energy by allowing yourself to breathe. You are cutting you off from life by judging life so harshly. Allow life to be. Allow you to be. Allow your neighbor to be. Allow your family to be. In doing so, you will be dropping the judgment habit and allowing you to simply "be"....

❧

*Y*ou will begin to understand the workings of your own thought process in due time. Most of you are in a place where you do not think; you "react." You do not stop and think why you are being triggered, you simply hear something or see something you do not like and you attack. You get angry and upset and you get all riled-up over the slightest little thing. This is due to the fact that you have been socialized and conditioned to *see* life a certain way. Once you let go of your *need* to have life look the way *you* have decided it should look, you will have more freedom. Right now you are locked into a specific pattern or way of viewing life. This way that you are locked into keeps you stuck in one particular reality when you could otherwise move up to a higher perspective, which would allow for you to be drawn into a higher vibrating wave or stream of energy.

Never forget that everything is energy. Never let go of your desire to go to the highest point. This is where you thrive. This is where you can truly be yourself. This is where spirit meets matter. This is where you will feel your wings. When you are in the highest vibrations, you are in a parallel reality that allows you to be free to choose without restraints placed on you. You are allowed to *receive* in a very big way. You are offered the gifts that are available to all of you humans who are taking part in this earth experience.

Most of you do not yet realize that you *are* the

creators of your reality. You know that you can change direction in life and create a better existence for yourself, but you have no idea as to how great an impact *you* have on how you see life and the world and the situations you live in, or avoid living in. You are so powerful and so unaware of your power. You are like an artist who does not know how to paint his very first painting. He sees the brushes and he sees the paints in their tubes, but no one has told him what to do with it all. He must experiment to learn that if he unscrews the cap on a tube of paint he can then *use* that paint on his canvas. He must experiment to know that the brushes in front of him can be *used* to add the paint to the canvas in various strokes. He must experiment to know that he can create images of great beauty by controlling his brushstrokes. And once in a while, he may learn to simply allow his hand the freedom to express the beauty that lies within his own self by "not" controlling his hand as it flows across the canvas.

You may gain great beauty and great joy by "not" controlling and by flowing with the energy of your life. If you are reading this book, you are more than likely a searcher of information that will guide you into a better way of existing for your own personal behavior. This book and the others that I have channeled through Liane are guidebooks to the more peaceful realms. If you are seeking a better way or as I would put it "a different way" of seeing your life and your world, you may decide that this information is what you are looking for. If, on the other hand, you are happy and content with your life, congratulations! Happy and content is a very good place to be. Allow yourself to exist in happiness and contentment by allowing yourself to exist in your perfect reality. Your perfect reality is where you will feel best. You will feel light and happy and full of love. You will not necessarily sit around hugging yourself and everyone else all day, however you will feel great! Not just good, but great!

This is where you wish to exist and this is what you wish to be drawn to. You all want to be loved and you all want to be happy and you all want to be out of pain and harms way. You may assist your own self in gaining these gifts that you so deserve. You may assist yourself by raising your thoughts up out of judgment. I do not say this lightly. Judgment is your biggest hurdle and judgment - rather lack of judgment - will set you free. If you can simply face every situation you come into contact with as though it is some sort of "gift" that is being presented to you in disguise, you will begin to rise "up" in a very big way. Let go of judgment and you will be letting go of your anchor. Your anchor holds you down on the bottom of the field. The existence you are searching for is at the top. Allow yourself the freedom to float. Allow yourself to go "up" by letting go of the judgments you hold against yourself and others. "Not so easy to do" - you shout! Yes, I agree, and so I have written many books to guide you and to assist in this process.

It's all an inside job you know? All that you see is being projected by you onto your own personal viewing screen that you call "your life." Allow "your life" to lighten up by allowing yourself to let go of the very dense energy of judgment. You can do this. You are part of God creating on this material plane. Let go and "allow" your life to unfold for you in beautiful, magical ways by simply "allowing" every situation to be seen as containing a gift.

⚜

*Y*ou will continue to see your life and your world through the eyes of a victim until you learn to release your hold on victimhood. Most of you believe that you have been hurt or harmed by life. This allows you to see life as a villain or as painful. You do not realize that life is not painful nor is it hurtful. Life is simply a projection of what is within you.

Now, I realize that this is a very difficult concept for you to grasp in your current reality; however, you will begin to see how this is true once you calm down the energy that runs through your body. You draw energy to you and you draw you to energy. You are made up of energy and your projections are made up of energy. You begin by becoming afraid of something, and your mind works on that fear and it begins to get your emotions involved. Once your emotions are involved, you begin to vibrate with emotional energy. This vibrating emotional energy begins to affect the people and the things around you. You literally have an effect on the world around you. You then begin to "believe" your emotions and you see something that you once feared as now being sinister or bad. You even label certain situations as evil.

Some of you do not realize the extent to which you have *created* a bad or sinister world for yourself. You live *in* your creations simply because you *feel* the energy that you are sending out from you. Once in a while you actually catch yourself, and you will begin to calm your fears and *allow* your fearful situations to "not be so blown out of proportion." You are doing this! You are creating love where there could be fear, and you are creating fear where there could be love. You may choose to change many situations in your own personal reality by simply letting go of your fears, and by allowing yourself to believe that life is not so dangerous. Danger is an illusion, as all is an illusion on this plane of reality. You decide where you will live by what you choose to be fearful of.

Some of you are so afraid of death that you find killing to be the epitome of evil. Killing is simply ending the illusion for another spirit. You find it so comforting to know that you can safely end the life of your beloved pet when it is suffering, and yet you scream "how horrifying" when someone ends the life of a family member who is suffering.

You find it entertaining to watch killing movies and yet you find it horrifying to see killing on your news. You feel that killing is evil, and yet you feel that killing is okay if it is to protect your country's boundaries. You feel that killing for greed is horrific, yet killing for love is good. You are so confused, and your confusion has created a very unstable reality for you. You are more afraid of death than you are of life, simply because you believe that "in death" you end. You do not end - not ever! You are energy and you will never, ever end.

So, get over your fears by letting them go and you will begin to free yourself of emotional storms. Your emotional storms will draw you into a reality that is filled with storm energy. Do you often feel like your life is painful and in turmoil? Let go of your fear and allow your life to calm down by allowing yourself to calm down. See *everything* as turning out well in the end and you will be assisting yourself in a very big way.

You will begin to see how your vibratory life is quite important to your joy and your well-being. The higher you go in vibration, the happier you will feel emotionally. On some level you already know this. You talk about being really down in the dumps or sad. You also talk about being up or lifting yourself "up" to better feelings. So, on some level of consciousness, you know! Now, when you lift yourself up, you usually do not realize that you are literally shifting up to the next energy level. When you are down and depressed you are in a lower vibrating stream of reality. You might say that the energy stream you are in is matched to your vibration. If you are low, or blue, or sad you shift down and that allows you to drop down into a lower vibrating wave or reality. Once you shift back up, you are then literally lifting yourself up to the next higher vibrating reality. You may lift yourself "up" or lower yourself "down" at any time by your choice of feelings.

Now, once you "decide" to feel bad about any given situation, you may reverse your decision and "decide" to feel good about it. Say you have just received news that your beloved husband has cheated on you with another. You may "decide" to be incredibly angry and drop down into lower vibrations for a time, or you may "decide" to stay high and allow your husband to act out whatever it is that he is acting out. You may "decide" to kill him, or you may "decide" to love him unconditionally.

All life is simply a choice - nothing more, nothing less! You live in a material world that is only there because you are projecting it. It is not real in that you are not seeing a true, solid reality. You are seeing a reality that shifts and changes with your moods and your strong feelings. You might say that you only see what you want to see. You see through your own personal perspective, and your own personal perspective is shaped by your fear or lack of fear. Fear is memory-based emotion. If you once felt pain you will remember exactly how you encountered your pain and you will then begin to avoid, or shun, or even hate the situation that caused your pain. As years go by, you accumulate energy around this pain and it becomes a very large wound. As time goes by, your wound becomes extremely sensitive and you do not allow the least little infraction, or movements, in the direction of the original cause of your wound.

You are wounded and you are walking around in a very, very sensitive state. You are so sensitive that no one can disagree with you or have a different perspective. You are literally being *run by fear*. Let go of your *need* to have it your way. *Your way* is based on a great big wound, or blocked energy "in you" that is currently making your choices, and literally pulling you down into the lower vibrational waves of reality. And what do you get in the lower vibrations? You get more of the same. And what do you get in the higher vibrations? You get more of the same. High vibrations are happiness, joy, love, peace, calm, respect. Low vibrations are unhappiness, sadness, hatred, violence and disrespect. Come "up" or go "down." It is not a matter of God giving or God taking away. God is always "in" you and always "aware" of your choices. You are part of God and God is part of you. God is creative energy. God *allows* you to create and will not interfere except upon request. God will work with you by gently reminding you what your choices are, and how you are able to decide on the best direction for your soul.

You are not here to be in emotional pain and physical pain. You are here to play in the material realms and to become *conscious* while on this material plane. You are here to be you. You are light energy and you have just now discovered your light switch. Your light switch is your emotional energy. Turn you on! Be love, be light! See the world through the filter of love and let go of your wounds by allowing them to heal. How do you heal a wound? You feed it medicine, and in this case that medicine would be forgiveness. I am not talking about inviting the worst into your life. I am talking about inviting the higher energies in to dissolve the lower energies. Fear disappears when love is present. The two simply cannot coexist. When you are in a state of love, you are in a state of "acceptance." You are open and available and willing to see and accept change. You allow change by allowing yourself to try something different. Why not try forgiveness and let go of your wounds and begin to heal.

I have written a twenty book series on this subject and if you feel you are ready to *see life differently* you may wish to read this most valuable information. For now, I will simply remind you to watch your feelings and notice where you are sensitive to the touch. This is where your pain lies and this is where you will *distort* the energy into something else. When you carry a rather large wound within you, you may turn a simple gesture by someone into a great affront. You are so accustomed to turning molehills into mountains and I would like to see you bring it down a notch. Wouldn't you like to be a little more "easy-going" in your life? After all, easy-going energy will draw you into an easy-going wave of energy or an easy-going reality.

You will soon begin to see how you do not require a great deal of energy to accomplish your goals. Once you begin to let go and go with the flow of the energy of your life, you will feel as though you might accomplish a great deal and with great ease. Most of you push yourselves to do more and to be more, however, you could simply ask spirit to move you in this direction or that direction. When you are working with spirit, spirit begins to assist you in many ways.

Say you have a physical activity you must accomplish. This could be as simple as cleaning the floor in your home or as complex as building a new room. Once you have decided on your goal you might ask spirit to be with you in this project. You might request the spirit *in* you to assist you and to guide you. First you must ask spirit to be present *in* you. Spirit has been ignored by you for most of your life. Imagine being a spirit that inhabits a body and never being allowed to take part in the human experience from a conscious perspective. Imagine not being allowed to consciously guide your human in its life here on earth. Imagine not being noticed and not being *felt* by the body that carries you. Imagine no recognition whatsoever. How would you feel if you were here to guide and love and take part in a lifetime, but no one knew you existed? No one sees you, no one hears you and no one talks to you.

I would like to take this opportunity to introduce you to your very own personal self. This is your soul... the spirit *in* you has been patiently waiting for you to wake up enough that you begin to communicate with it. Yes! The spirit *in* you is part of you and it is the part of you that never ever dies. It is the part of you that is eternal. It is the part of you that is God. Do you want to know this part of you? Do you want to communicate with this part of you? Do you want to become friends with the spirit *in* you, or do you fear all things paranormal and unknown to the physical senses? Do you want to be part of something greater than your body and your mind? I do hope you wish to meet with and move with spirit at some point.

The spirit in you is the part of you that is most ignored and is also most powerful. You may be guided by and moved by spirit once you have *reconnected* with your own soul. Your soul lives *in* you and your soul is not an organ. It does not exist in just one place in you. It exists in every cell of your body and it is the energy that is light awareness. It is the intelligence of the universe and this intelligence is in every cell of your body. You are permeated with light awareness and God intelligence, and you simply do not know that you are.

How can this be? How can you have this huge part of you that is alive *in* you and you have no relationship with it? You may worship God and pray to God and the angels, but you do not know *consciously* that you are God. You are not consciously aware of your individual divinity and how your individual divinity is the most powerful, beautiful, loving part of you. You might say that "you are a diamond in the rough." You are magnificent and unconscious of this fact.

As you move to a place of acceptance of yourself and all that exists, I wish you to *remember* who you are. I wish you to accept yourself just as you are and to accept life just as it is. When you judge, you block the flow of energy to you. I'm sure you have heard the phrase "his spirit was crushed," or "her spirit was killed by that experience." Usually your spirit is alive and well *in* you, however, you may block spirit by going deeper into unconsciousness. You go deeper into unconsciousness by *judging*. Judgment blocks the energy *in* you from flowing freely. Judgment dams you up and shuts you down. Be unafraid to accept life "as is." If you can begin to calm yourself down enough to stop jumping to conclusions about how awful your circumstances are, you will allow "acceptance" to take hold in your life. You will then be "accepting" all parts of life (even the paranormal parts) and you will draw yourself into a reality wave of acceptance. How can you accept the gifts of life if you live in the energy of judgment? Judgment pushes life away. Acceptance brings life and all the gifts of life to you.

You will be accepting life and you will be accepting *you*. Now, look down at your body. I would like to formally introduce you to the spirit that resides in every cell of *you*. Please be kind and loving and *accepting* of this part of you.

⚜

*Y*ou will soon begin to change how you view yourself

and how you view the world. Most of what you now see as painful, or wrong, will begin to dissolve away as you see how life is simply energy that is moving and flowing. You will begin to let go of your "why me" mentality and you will begin to allow for change more readily.

Once you can "accept" that life is actually a giant flow of energy and that this giant flow of energy is in constant movement, you will begin to see how you can work "with" this energy, or, you can fight and struggle to change this energy. If you choose to flow with the energy, you may be moved into a flow that is much calmer. It is similar to floating with the current of water. You may be like a fish that is fighting to go upstream or you may flow with the current and end up downstream. Once you are floating you are much calmer. Once you are calmer it is easier for you to adapt and accept change. Once you adapt and accept change, you are less fearful of change. Since "change" is what life is all about, it is good to be changeable or flexible.

You are often in a position to change and, out of your own fear of change, you insist on changing everyone else or the world around you. You do not like change and your fear regarding change is causing a few problems for you. When you *accept* change, you literally *allow* yourself to join the *flow of life*. Life is constantly changing and flowing, and you are frightened and holding on tight to your old ways and old habits. Try balance! Try to let go enough that you move a little with the flow of life. Try to let go a little here and a little there, until you are no longer stuck in your *fear of letting go.*

Once you get to a place where change is acceptable to you, you will be drawing yourself into a wave of energy that is changing and growing. How can you change your circumstances if you constantly think your way is the only way, and you are so stubborn that you will not change you? You are spending all of your time and energy trying to change the world and people around you. The one who requires changing is you. The only reason you *require* changing is because you said so. How did you say you *require* changing? You said "they" need to change or fix how "they" do this or that.

It is not possible to change *you* by changing them. If you want *them* to behave differently then change your behavior. You draw yourself into a wave of reality that will *reflect* to you exactly what you carry *in* you. If you carry judgment you will judge absolutely everything, and nothing *in* life will be good enough. This draws you into a reality where you are judging everyone and everything as not good enough.

Have you lost faith in people? Have *you* decided that the world has gone beyond saving? Be very careful and watch how you judge. You are simply "seeing" what is "in" you and what makes you tick. If you see no hope for life and the world, you have literally given up on *you* and find yourself to be hopeless. You are not hopeless and you are not un-savable. You are the creative force of energy that makes up God! You are as divine as God, and you are an individual divine spark that is off on its own *creating* as God. Do not give up on you. Do not give up on life, as life is simply the movie that *you* have projected yourself into in an effort to see who and what you are. If you are in a movie (life) that is not to your liking do not judge it, move on into a movie that you enjoy. You are an energy being existing in an energy field.

Do not be so hard on yourself and on others. You are all moving and changing, and most of you are afraid and holding on to harsh judgments regarding life and people.

Let your judgments go and *allow* yourself to flow....

≈≋≈

*A*s far as you can see from where you now stand, you are in an energy world of your own making. How is it possible that you could be so unaware of how you create and project your creations? If you are not looking at an object is it still there where you first saw it? You look at a vase of flowers and it is right in front of you, and you see the beauty and you smell the fragrance. What happens when you turn around and look the other way? Does your bouquet continue to look the same, or is there another layer of reality there where your flower vase stands?

Could it be that there is another dimension where you are, that is maybe a train station that literally runs through your living room? Could it be that there are passengers and people who are on their way to a new adventure, and they are lined up in your *now* living room boarding this train? Could it be that your flower vase is where they sit on the train, and when you are not *aware* of it, this train will leave the station in this other dimension that is layered above your dimension? Could it be that you have so much to learn about time and space and consciousness? Could it be that you are the masters of this fictitious world that you live in, and you are totally unaware of your role?

You are not living in a multi-verse so much as you are living in a painting that has layer, upon layer, upon layer of existence, only none of it is real. It is all projected onto the screen that you call life. You are projecting all of this and it is very much like a movie, and you are simply playing a game with yourself and the other gods who create this illusion right along with you.

So, why do I tell you this and not explain how to come out of this dream that you live in? I am trying to explain to you in terms that you can understand. The first step to becoming conscious is to wake up to the fact that it is not real, it is not dangerous and no one ever dies. If you could just get that part through the filters of your mind, you will be in a better position to heal and to wake up. No one ever dies. No one ever ends. There are no bad guys. There are no bad choices and nothing is wrong. God does not rule over you and punish you. You are God and you create it all.

Yes! There is God awareness outside of your tiny focal point of awareness, however, that God awareness is not a boss nor a tyrant, nor a king, nor a ruler, nor a punisher of your sins. There are no sins as there is no wrong way to create. How can you call anything wrong when it is all a big illusion and does not really exist? Why do I write this to you now? Because I wish you to calm down and begin to see peace. How can you create from a position of peace when your mind and your emotions are in a constant state of turmoil? You are creating by projection. It comes from within you and you are receiving back exactly what you put out.

It's all energy, people! And you are creating in the blind and then you blame life and so life is now a villain. You want a good and happy life, so I strongly suggest that you stop all blame and judgment. Just stop! Calm down and breathe. Breathe in and breathe out and think peaceful thoughts. You will be calming yourself down, which will calm your life down, which will calm the energy down, which will make life easier and more pleasurable for you.

I do not ask you to calm down because I am God and I want you to be good children. I ask you to calm down because you are so afraid of life that you are literally turning it into something hard and scary and dangerous. You began going into various dimensions as a way to discover yourself and your ability to exist on many levels at the same time. You have now gotten stuck in your little game and you believe it is real. This is not the real you! The real you is love and acceptance and light. You are the *light* and now you cower in darkness and fear. Come out of the shadows and begin to see everything as light! You will find that the more light you can shed on your life and your world, the greater light you will be adding to your world. It all begins and ends with you. Turn up the light! Dial up the peace! It begins and ends with you. You can do this. Begin to see how you *decide* what everything is by what you call it. Simply stop calling it all bad and begin to call it good or just okay. From "okay" you can easily make the shift up to the next higher vibration of good.

~ ❧ ~

*Y*ou are at a turning point in your evolution and you may decide to go in a whole new direction. This is a time of change and it is important for you to be flexible in your thinking. Allow for change by accepting diversity. Diversity is big because diversity *allows* for any possibility. Since you do not yet know who you are and what makes you tick, it would be a good idea to accept all possibilities.

So, if you do turn out to be God, how will you handle your new identity? If you turn out to be divine, how will you *perceive* your reality? How does it make you feel to *know* that you are God/creative power? How do you feel about being *responsible* for *your* creations? You do it all, you know? You are this higher power that you speak about in hushed tones. So how do we get you to see how you create your circumstances without blaming you for creating your circumstances? We allow you to learn just a little at a time how to *change* your behavior, in order to change your circumstances.

The greatest gift you can give yourself is the gift of gratitude. Gratitude allows you to change your circumstances with little effort on your part. Most of what occurs when you feel grateful is quite satisfying for you, as gratitude often puts a smile on your face. When you are grateful, you are thankful. Thankfulness is an energy of joy and happiness. If I ask you to be happy and joyful you will be stumped; especially if you are in an unappreciative mood. What if instead of asking you to be happy and joyful I simply say, "Be thankful for that tree outside your window?" Or maybe I might remark on how nice it is to be able to *see* that tree outside your window. Immediately your sense of gratefulness kicks in and raises your level of energy. This is how you will dig yourself out of any hole that you have fallen into energetically. You will raise yourself up by using gratefulness and thankfulness.

Do not forget about this powerful tool that you have

at your disposal. You may move up into the higher vibrating frequencies by allowing your gratitude to run wild and take over your life. This is the strongest force that you may use at this time. I know that love is the highest vibration; however, you have so much confusion around love and what love is. I have written an entire book on how to love yourself which may be of help to you. It is titled *The Book of Love*. If you read *The Book of Love* you may find yourself in a position to *accept* your own love of self on a much higher level. You will find that this material will change and grow as you change and grow.

The information that is coming to earth at this time is meant to assist in this waking up process that you are going through. You will find that a great deal of information is relatable from various levels of consciousness. As you grow in awareness, you may go back and reread information and it will make sense to you in a whole new way. Often information is *perceived* by the reader from the level where the reader lives. As the reader raises their level of consciousness, they will be allowed to see greater insights in the messages that have been given.

Repetition is also a great tool for you to use. If you can tell yourself over and over and over again how wonderful life is, you will begin to believe it. In the same way that you can program yourself to believe that life is awful or dangerous; you can program yourself to believe that life is a great big giant gift to you from you.

*A*s you continue to feel grateful and thankful I wish you to begin to *see* how you are part of everything. It is not easy for you to see the connection between yourself and your neighbor. You are actually part of the same being. Some of you see yourselves as part of your loved ones; however, you find it quite difficult to see yourself as part of a stranger or even a relative whose beliefs are far removed from your own.

You are each part of the whole that is the creative energy that permeates absolutely everything. Nothing is left out and no one is left out. So, how do you become someone who sees themselves as separate from the whole? You begin to split and to separate, until you have split and separated so much that you no longer know who you are, or where you came from. You might see yourself as a long-lost relative, or sibling, who was separated from their family at birth but never told that they were. They now live on opposite sides of the world, and were raised in different environments and have completely different views of the world and life and reality. You may meet this sibling in your travels and you may not recognize them as part of your family.

So, does this make them less lovable and acceptable? Does the fact that you do not consciously know that they are part of your family make them any less a part of your family? *You are all one being and you are all unconscious regarding this fact.* You walk this earth and you judge one another and you are separate only in thought and belief. You make up the body of this giant everlasting being that we will call God. You sit here in your ignorance and your blindness, and you do not have a clue as to who you are and who they are, so please stop judging you and stop judging them. You really need to stop! Not because it is wrong, but because you are a creative *force,* and you are unaware of your power to create and your ability to hold you *down.*

You have been lower than you wish to be and it is time now to raise your focus. Do not look down unless you wish to go in that direction. Energy follows thought. Do not think low, think high... focus up! Not only will you raise yourself "up," you will be sending energy out into the universe that is uplifting.

So, if you find yourself down in the dumps with low energy, just remember that you are divine and part of God. Ask yourself, "what would God do," or "what is good for your soul," and do that. What is good for your soul is good for the whole. You are part of a giant being that is the creative force of all life. How do you think it would be to have one tiny cell, within the body of this giant being, who cannot accept itself and therefore not accept others? Learn to trust. Learn to accept and begin to *see* the bigger picture. This will bring you up a little higher in your vibration, which adds a little bit higher vibration to the entire being that you are part of. Do not judge the other cells in the body, as you are so unconscious that you do not *realize* the effect you may have on them as a whole, and on yourself as an individual soul, or cell within the body of God.

❧

*T*he most important part of your life is how you *perceive* your life. Many of you see your life as not good enough and you wish you had more, and bigger, and better. This is not the best way to view your life. The best way to view your life is to see the *value* in being *you*. See how valuable you are and you will see how you add value to your world. See how valuable you are, and you will be moving yourself into a reality that is truly valuable.

So, how do we see ourselves as valuable when we have low self-esteem and we do not look valuable in our own eyes? We begin to see ourselves as part of God. It is not easy to see yourselves as part of God when you do not see yourself as valuable, so now we will change this to "see yourself as divine." Oh, I see, you do not see yourself as divine. So now we will ask you to see yourself as a spiritual being. Can you do that? Can you see yourself as a spiritual being? If you are a spiritual being, what is your purpose? How do you get here? Why do you come and what is your purpose? What if your purpose is to simply exist? What if this entire experience was simply a test to see if energy (spiritual energy) could enter and sustain stability within a human form? What if the only reason you came here to earth was to *exist* in matter and allow matter to eventually *feel* your presence? What if you were part of a giant creation experiment that was set in movement by God expressing and giving off energy?

What if you are this God energy and what if you are part of the divine energy that makes up God? Would you feel better about yourself if you knew that you were/are a divine spirit within a human body? Would you feel better about yourself if you knew that the energy that runs through your cells is God? Would you feel better about who you are if you suddenly became *aware* of the fact that God rides around inside of you day and night? Would it help you to love you more if you could see the God in you? Would it take you into a better life, or feeling about your life, if you were consciously *aware* that you are divine and that God lives *in* you day in and day out? Would you then be a little kinder to you and with your thoughts about yourself?

You are a divine spirit and you exist within a human body. You are the best, most wonderful, most creative energy and you think you have no value. You are the most valuable of all. You are all little pieces of the whole, and the whole is the body of God. Your job is to be part of God and you do it well. You simply are unaware that you each make up God, and so you have little to no respect for who you are. You want the gifts of this life and you want wealth and meaning, and I will tell you now that the meaning of your life is to be God in human form. Do not worry about what you see, as you can change what you see. It is as easy as changing the channel on your television. You may choose to see war and violence, or you may choose to see love and peace. It is all simply part of the God within human experience. You made it in! You are here! Now it is time to wake up to who you are and exactly how valuable you truly are.

Celebrate! Celebrate yourself because being you is really something to celebrate. Your individual divinity has survived and is strong within you. It is growing and expanding, and you are becoming *aware* that there is more to you than flesh and bones. You are much, much more! You are divine in nature and you are from God! You are part of the creative energy that allows for All That Is to be All That Is. You are greater than you currently see and you are waking up bit by bit to your own greatness. Can you feel it? Do you have those moments? Those moments of insight will increase bit by bit, until you are more conscious of who you are than your current unconscious state.

Hold on! Do not give up on you, for if you do you will be giving up on the God in you. You have great value just by your presence and your existence. You are the best of life. You are God in a body. It doesn't get better than that!

⚬✿⚬

*A*s you continue to see yourself as more than simply a human being, I wish you to remember to be very loving and kind to the spirit that resides within your body. You are part of your own creation, and you are part of God the creator of All That Is.

You will find that the greater your ability to be kind to yourself, the greater your ability to show kindness to the world and to life. You are in a position whereby you might direct your energy in various ways, and you may also affect the energy of this universe that you call home. Most of the time, you are in a state of worry concerning survival and acceptance and fitting in. When you are in a state of concern over how you will do in the future, you affect this present moment in a very big way.

Say you have a home and you are constantly worried about finances and how you will keep your home. This fear energy will go out from you as an energy vibration, or frequency. You now will be sending an energy out from you that says, "Someone will take my home from me." This does not mean that you will lose your home to someone else, however, it does send a strong signal of energy that has the message "take my home from me" in it. It might be better to see you keeping your home in the future by not worrying and by allowing thoughts of a more positive nature. You could envision you living in your home in old age, or you could envision yourself being happy and healthy in old age. Either of these latter thoughts would raise your vibration and allow you to magnetize a higher wave of energy.

When you worry, you automatically bring yourself down. When you expect the worst it is like expecting a package in the mail. You will eventually see your future through your expectations. Expect only the best! Allow yourself to focus on the positive and you will be allowing yourself to join the positive energy forces. No one is out to get you or to punish you by taking away your gifts. You present yourself with gifts by *allowing* yourself to rise up to the highest vibrations. Think of energy as a gift. Think of your thoughts and emotions as a gift. Think of your ability to affect your life as a gift. You are a gift! Your life is a gift! You get to decide the kind of person you want to be, and you get to decide if worry is what you want to live in, or if peace of mind is where you prefer to be.

Do not fear. The worst that can happen is change. We are not talking life and death here; and even if we are there is no such thing as death. You simply change back to spirit, take off your costume, and leave the play, or movie, you were acting so well in. You move back to the energy flows that suit you, and you continue on your way of expressing, and experimenting, and enjoying being divine spirit or God force. You never end so you cannot lose. You are divine energy. Life is good! You are great and wonderful, and the only problem in this whole wide world is your inability, at this time, to see how divine and wonderful absolutely everything is....

❀

*Y*ou are probably concerned about how your future will play out and you are more than likely wondering how your relationships will go. I will tell you now that the best way to have a bright future is to *see* a bright today. No doom and gloom please. No concern for events that may or may not occur. If you want your future to be bright, I do hope you are projecting a *bright* present moment.

You do not need to convince everyone of your worries and your concerns. You may see the world and life as falling apart, but please, do not spread *your* interpretation, as your interpretation is coming from *within* you and is colored by your past experience, and your mental beliefs, and your personal fears. If you wish to convince others to see your point of view and it is less than bright, I would highly suggest that you stop. Just stop and get calm and breathe. Do not spread negativity unless you wish to subject yourself to greater negativity.

Now, if you see destruction and war and violence, I wish you to see your world as coming out of such dense energies. If you see political corruption, I wish you to see this moving your country to a much better place. Always see life as improving and your life will slowly begin to improve. Do not dwell on the negative as it will cause you to spiral downward, and you will be digging yourself into a dark hole. You will enter realities that are dense by constantly viewing life as dense. See the light and see the good and see the love whenever possible. See your life as an adventure that you get to share with other adventurers. Go into life with your eyes wide open, and with the acute *awareness* that *you* have the ability to *shift* your life into a position of positivity and light.

Go into your life with the awareness that you create life situations, and then you change what you have created by how you *perceive* what you are looking at. Have you ever seen a picture or painting that holds a hidden picture or painting within it? This is where you are. You are so confused by your ability and your power to create that you see the least little thing as a threat. You see life as going downhill and so your life turns in that direction. If you can just find the positive, or even let go of the negative, long enough to allow the downward energy to slow down, you will have a good chance at seeing the positive or at least a neutral perspective.

If you cannot see life as good, at least see it is okay. If you cannot see life as okay, then I highly suggest you stop all judgment and heal yourself. You do not need to heal your neighbor; you do require self-help and healing.

So, if you can *allow* everything to be okay, you will slow down the downward pull that you have inflicted upon yourself. I'm sure you have all seen on your news, or maybe read about, doomsdayers who constantly worry about the worst end result or scenario. Then we have those who thrive and are happy, and know that everything will eventually work out for the best. How hard do you fight and argue to let those, who see everything as okay and all right just as things are, know that they are wrong and your perspective is right?

Here's the thing… I am God and I am trying to get through the dense energy that you have surrounded yourself with, in order to let you know that everything is okay. Not only is it okay, it is better than okay. You are so stuck in your fears that you cannot, or will not, believe me. Please begin to see the light and come out of this darkness that you insist on holding on to. You are like a "hoarder" and no one can convince you to "let go" of the stuff you are holding on to. Why? Simply because you are afraid of what will become of you if you let go of all this "stuff" you hold tight to. And what is happening to you as a result of being a hoarder of negative views? You get to see more and more negativity. It's time to clean up this mess and allow the *light* to shine on you once again. Hoarding can cause many problems, and can suffocate you under that huge load of debris and denseness.

Come home to the light. Let go of *your* need to create greater fear, and let go of *your* desire to have everyone else "see it your way."

꧁꧂

Whenever you begin to feel like your life is not as good as it should be, I would like you to consider the fact that life is simply an extension of mind. Mind is perception, and perception is what you create from. Life is literally the reflection that is projected out for your eyes to see and your mind to evaluate.

Begin to give good, positive evaluations of life and you will be *changing* your view of life. Change your view of life and you change your stance, or where you stand on the subject of your life. You may change your view at any time by changing how you "perceive" or "judge" everything around you. Think of yourself as a mound of clay that has come alive and is being molded into a conscious life form. This mound of clay is being created every day and shaped into a living form. The form that this mound of clay takes is determined by the energy that is being run through the clay.

If this clay is too dry, it becomes brittle and dried out and it develops cracks. If, on the other hand, this clay is too moist it will become soft and mushy and not hold firm.

So, you would like this clay to be firm and yet flexible enough to work with. This is how I would like to see you become - firm and yet flexible. Allow for change and allow yourself to be molded into a beautiful work of art. Most of you do not like change and you are not so very good at being flexible. You may be very flexible in one or two areas of your life and yet you are very stuck in other areas.

You most often do not relate to those who behave differently, or think differently, or live differently. You find it difficult to *trust* anyone who is too different from yourself. This is about to change. I want you to observe how others react to life and to accept that differences are a good thing. I want you to come to a place where you can allow for big differences, and begin to *understand* that the same energy that runs through you runs through them. You are the same God energy and yet you hate them and their ways. You come from God, you have a soul or spirit that is directly connected to God, and yet you find them intolerable.

You will learn that most of your intolerances come from your own personal experiences and fears. Most of your fears come from a place of pain or a deep, old wound. You may have been shot in a past life and now you fear guns. This may cause you to be totally opposed to any laws allowing firearms. You may have gotten so angry in a past life that you shot and killed someone. This may affect you in this particular life and you may judge others who kill harshly, as you are still judging yourself for killing in a past life.

This is how time works. It is not real. There really is no past and yet this is how it *appears* to you. You see time as linear and so I will speak with you as though time is linear.

Once you come into a new life you bring with you all of your experiences from past lives. So, if you hated what you did or how you did it in a past life, you may bring that judgment energy forward into this life. Now you have this life compounded by this life's experiences as well as past life experiences. How can you *decide* what is acceptable in this life when you are being bombarded with energy judgment from past life, as well as from this life? It is most difficult and often very confusing for each of you.

Then I come along and begin to explain for you how you have never done "wrong" except *in your own judgment*. Now you must decide just how to think and what to believe, and you have all those past experiences and judgments that have shaped this you into who you are.

The easiest way to let go of past judgments is to stay calm and *observe*. Do not take sides! Allow yourself to simply watch and allow yourself to become *aware* of the fact that this is just a movie, a play that is being acted out for enjoyment, pleasure and entertainment. You are not seeing reality. You are seeing a "chosen" reality. This is one of many and you may choose to see a new movie by changing the way you "perceive" your current movie. See it as good fun and interesting. Then you will begin to "shift" the energy in the direction of "fun and interesting."

You are not the only one who is confused and judging your current reality. You may, however, be one of the first to come up out of confusion and enter the realms of awareness.

෴

When you come into consciousness, you begin to *feel* different about everything. Once you regain consciousness, you will no longer fear life and you will no longer fear results created by you or by others. Once you regain consciousness, you will find it easy to love everything and everyone. Consciousness is a wonderful state of being and it will bring you great joy and comfort. Right now you live in discomfort and pain. Most of you exist in a state of emotional pain and many exist in a state of physical pain. Most pain is brought on by a breakdown within the cellular system and is always fixable through the cellular system.

Most pain is brought on by a lack of connection with your energy source. The less connection, the greater the blocks within the system. Once you open up and end the blockages within you, you will find it much easier to stay happy and healthy. Most of you do not realize that you contain these blockages, and so you spend your life blaming God or blaming life for your illnesses and your health problems. Health problems may be brought forward from past life or they may be created within a single lifetime.

Health problems are always due to energy blocks within the cellular system. If you wish to know which problems are brought on by which energy blocks, I highly suggest you read "You Can Heal Your Body" by Louise Hay. This little book is packed with powerful insights into how *you* create problems by your thoughts and beliefs. I highly recommend it as a wonderful guide into *you* and how you operate.

Now, once you have discovered where your blockages lie, you may then begin to raise your level of awareness, and this will allow you to create a smoother ride through life. You need not know everything to gain a pleasurable life; however, it is good to have some *awareness* of how *you* create.

As you continue to raise your level of consciousness, you will wish to learn how you create relationship problems for yourself. Most relationship problems are caused by a lack of trust and a fear of loss! Most relationship problems are a result of low self-esteem and fear. You fear losing and you fear being alone and you fear not being accepted; and I will tell you now that acceptance *is* love. If you cannot accept someone you cannot possibly show that person love. If you cannot accept them unconditionally you do not love them unconditionally.

Allow your loved ones to be who they are and stop trying to make them into another you. You are not faring so well in your awareness, so why would you want to bring them into your state of unconsciousness with you? They may be light years ahead of you in some areas, and you come along and begin to push them to do more and be more like you. Leave my children alone and tend to your own garden. You think that you are in the know and smarter than those you claim to love, and you are not smarter on a spiritual scale. You are simply different. They are just as spiritual whether they recognize God or not. They are just as aware whether they discuss it with you or not. You are not above anyone, and I wish you would focus on you and let the rest of my children be.

So, what does this all have to do with existing in parallel realities? It is how you exist that affects where you exist within this vastness of energy. You wish to raise your level of awareness in an effort to raise you up to a much "lighter" reality. You get there by "lightening up." Do not bring others down by judging them as not as smart as you are, because you will be sending you to stupidville. You will send you where ever you send them. If you believe your spouse to be stupid you run the message "you are stupid" through "your" body every time you have that thought or think that way. If you see your brothers and sisters as idiots, it is the same thing as if you were to call yourself an idiot. Why? Simply because you are the one judging the situation and the judgment is strong energy that runs through the cells *in* your body. You affect you with every thought you think.

Think kindness at all times and you will be running kindness through your body at all times. Focus on you not on them. Let them be who they are. "Live and let live" is a very good motto to live by.

⁂

*Y*ou will begin to understand your ability to create

once you begin to *observe* your creations. In your day-to-day living you may observe how you stir things up out of fear and how you calm things down out of love.

Love is the way to go if you desire peace and joy. Fear is the way to go if you desire conflict and anger. You are so afraid of war and conflict and yet you *desire* the excitement it brings. Even in your personal relationships you become bored when things get too calm and peaceful. Some of you were literally raised in chaos and you are uncomfortable if you do not create enough stimulation in your personal life. You feel bored and unimportant if you are not stirring things up.

Here is the secret to joy and peace - live a calm life. Live in peace and you will know peace. So, "what's the fun in that?" - you ask. I will tell you... you are always going to find what you are looking for. If you are searching for excitement, you will find excitement. If you are looking for calm you will find calm. If you are looking for an argument you will find an argument, and if you are looking for love and acceptance, you will find love and acceptance.

You need not fight with others to gain love and acceptance. Love and acceptance come from giving out love and acceptance. You may give to others or you may give to yourself. It does not matter who you give it to, it only matters that you are sending the energy of love and acceptance through your body and your cells. When you send love and acceptance through the cells in your body they literally begin to relax and to calm down. You might think of this as a way of de-stressing *you*. And we all know how stress can bring on illness and all kinds of health problems, including hair falling out and hair turning gray.

So, let go of stress by *allowing* yourself to send the energy of love and acceptance through your body and your cells. Your cellular structure will calm down and this means *you* will calm down. When you are calm, you do not feel like fighting and you do not feel so fearful. When you are calm, you are relaxed and not so stiff. When you are calm you are peaceful. If this sounds boring to you, you may want to look at why you are *drawn* towards conflict. Some of you *believe* that you require stimulation to not get bored with life, and you will find that you constantly create situations of chaos in your life. If your life feels chaotic and you would like it to slow down, I highly suggest you begin to love and accept yourself in an effort to calm your cellular structure. This will allow you to become relaxed, which will allow you to slow down and breathe.

Once you have slowed down, I wish you to take life easy and to continue to see peace by allowing peace to reign within you.

***

When you are judging yourself and others, you are creating dense energy. Dense energy goes down and light energy rises. The lighter the energy that you give off the higher you go in the field of energy that you exist within.

So, if you wish to stay high then I suggest you give off lighter energy waves. These energy waves that you give off will draw you up into the lighter energy realities. Creating is really quite simple once you get the hang of it. Joy will bring you greater joy and sorrow will bring greater sorrow. Anger creates more anger, frustration creates more frustration. If you want love, send love, if you want happiness and kindness, send happiness and kindness. If you wish to see criticism and sarcasm in your world then be sure to send out lots of criticism and sarcasm. It's all just energy and it will lift you up into a new reality or lower you down to a new reality. You get to determine where you go and how long you stay.

Now, I wish to discuss manifestation. Some of you have tried and tried to *create* wealth and/or prosperity for yourselves and you feel that you have failed miserably. Why not *allow* creation to come to you without being so strict as to what you wish for. If you constantly tell God; the field; your source; a higher power to give you something specific you are really locking yourself into one tiny possibility out of billions of possibilities. Ask for happiness and allow for many more possibilities to arrive. This will take less time to manifest and you will know exactly what you are getting. If you require security simply focus on and begin to *believe* that you are safe and secure, and you will be raised into a wave of energy or a reality where safe and secure exists. Remember... anger gets more anger; joy brings you into more joy. So what is "safe and secure" going to bring you? Right - you get more of what you put out.

Do not focus on what you fear! Do focus on what you love. Love and fear are two opposing energies and you cannot feel them simultaneously. You must choose. Do you wish to live in a life and a reality created from fear energy, or do you wish to live in a life and a reality created from love? This is how you learn to create and to *use* your power. You are gifted with the power of creation because you are part

God. You are part human, however you are becoming more God by the simple fact that you are waking up and becoming aware. As you wake and become aware, you literally *open up* to *receive* more God energy.

Everything is actually God and nothing is left out of God, however, you are allowing God to use your body by allowing yourself to wake up and to rise up. God is such a high energy that is undiluted and omnipotent, that it is impossible for you in matter to directly *receive* all that God is. God must be presented to you in small doses until you are stretched (for lack of a better word) enough to take on more light. You have been taking on light now for some time and you are being raised up in an effort to join God. You and God are one, and on an energy level you have distorted yourself to the point that you are unrecognizable as God. You, however, are now returning to God and taking on the role you were originally meant to play.

When you were originally created as spirit, you decided to move away and change into whatever form you might decide suited you at that time. Now you are coming home, and you are going to take off your costume and leave this game that you have been playing with yourselves. It is only a game and it was meant as fun; however, you have lost your sense of humor with this game called "Life in Human Form," and so you are going to wake up and snap out of it, and know that you are simply a spirit acting out a role.

Once you come out of the role you are currently playing, you may choose a new role or you may choose to move on to new endeavors. You are then able to assist in other areas of manifestation and creation. For now, you are in the process of waking up and coming out of the dream (which has turned into a disturbing nightmare for some) and you are going to realize that you are the creator of your current reality.

Once we get you to see *how* you create, we will work on getting you to calm down and *accept* life so that you might embrace life. Once you embrace life, you can more easily "let go and let God take over." You are beginning to wake up by accepting and receiving the God *in* you, and next you will accept and receive all/everyone/everything as part of you....

*Y*ou will begin to see great change in your world and in your life as you learn to use your power wisely. Your power is your ability to create. Your ability to create is a divine gift and is built into you. You may create blindly and unawarely or you may create consciously and with great vision. If you *decide* to create with awareness, you will see that your power is like a muscle, the more you use it, the stronger it gets. The less you use it the more lax it gets.

So, if you wish to see great change in your world and in your life, I highly suggest you begin to work with and become *aware* of your ability to create. You may start small by constantly watching where your thoughts go. Do they go "up" to the lighter energies of joy, love and acceptance or do they go down to the lower energies of sorrow, fear and judgment?

Once you *realize* how often your thoughts draw your

feelings "down," you may find it easier to stop them in midstream and direct them back "up" to lighter feelings and hence, lighter waves of energy. Remember - everything is already alive and in existence in the field of energy that encompasses All That Is. You simply move in and out of various levels of energy depending on which you are drawn towards. You are like a magnet and you draw to you that which you contain. If you do not wish to see lack and loss, begin to see your life as full and plentiful. If you do not wish to see pain and suffering, see your life as pain-free and happy. Begin to see your life as always improving.

Many of you reach a certain age and you begin to see everything as going downhill, and you begin to see your life as simply a waiting game to die. Begin to see your life as full and vibrant and ahead of you, not behind you. See your life as thriving and you will then be creating a thriving experience. See your life as full of possibilities and you will be creating all possibilities. See your life as new instead of old. You tend to begin to dull your excitement and enthusiasm for life with each year that passes. When you are young you look forward to the next day as though it is an adventure. As you get older you decide you know everything, and so you *block* new experiences and hence, new energy from coming into your experience. You fear change and you do not trust change. When you are young you love change and you actually *thrive* on change. So, what happens to you that you no longer embrace change? You grow afraid and nervous and defensive, and you believe that life has gotten the best of you and beaten you down. Life has only done what you told it to do! Fear has polluted the energy of your life.

Here is the truth - you are not living a life of joy and love and acceptance when you are busy judging and criticizing life and your neighbors and everything that you see. You *are* creating huge waves of fear energy that draw you into fearful realities. You live where your beliefs take you. Begin to "lighten up" regarding your view of life and you will once again see the world and life as "light." Let go of your need to live in fear and allow yourself to rise up to a more utopian view of life.

Let the denser energies go! They are coloring your world gray and dismal. Allow your world to be bright and fun and enjoyable. My pen has a favorite affirmation that I will share with you here. It goes like this, "Each and every day, I am better and better in every way!" I would suggest that you use something like this to assist in reprogramming your beliefs about your life. You may even change it a little to, "Each and every day my life is better and better in every way." I don't care if your life *feels* like the exact opposite. As a matter of fact, if your life *feels* like the exact opposite, I suggest you write this affirmation at least 100 times every morning. This will begin to shift the neurons into a new position, and they will eventually wire and connect differently within your brain.

Everything is an inside job and everything is about you healing and changing. Nothing is what you believe it to be. You have driven yourself into a dismal and often depressing state of mind. The good news is that you can turn around and drive yourself right back out!

*Y*ou will find that the easiest way to let go of judgment, criticism and anger is to be kind. Kindness and a generous spirit go a long way in alleviating any problems you may have. Kindness and generosity of spirit are the cornerstones of love. Kindness and generosity of spirit applies to you as well as your neighbor. You cannot be kind to you if you are not having kind thoughts towards them. You cannot feel love when you are feeling disgust and dissatisfaction. You cannot feel generous when you are withholding your acceptance.

You will find that a generous spirit is a giving spirit. Give your high vibration energy out whenever and wherever you can. High vibrational energies such as joy, pleasure, kindness, gratitude, acceptance and love will *always* support you and raise you up. Those energies run through your body and affect *you* in a very big way. These energies then go out and circle your planet and yes, they have a planetary effect as well. You may have heard stories of people who speak lovingly to their plants and even go so far as to play soothing music for them. This is energy at work.

Every time you send out a little positive, uplifting energy it has an effect on absolutely everything. So, be sure to send these positive, uplifting energies through your body daily. If you feel down, find a way to give good positive thoughts by focusing on something you love. Remember to always focus on what you love, not on what you hate or dislike. The more you focus on what you don't like, the greater the chance of lowering your self instead of raising your self. This is the whole premise behind heaven and hell.

Man gets many of his teachings confused and begins to go off on tangents regarding what is real, and what is truth, and what is illusion.

Basically you live in a world of illusion and you are creating it as you go. You are even creating God as you go. All energy is being multiplied and divided and expanded. And since you live and exist *within* All That Is, you are part of All That Is. As you grow and experience and expand, you literally send all energy back to the field of All That Is, which you exist within. You are God and you are growing and expanding through your awareness and spirit energy. You might say that you are like a giant balloon that is being inflated and thereby, expanded. Once expansion ends you then begin to deflate and let out all the energy (air) you took in. You are at the point of deflation and it is time to let go of a few things.

One of the things that will assist you as you "let go" is to realize, or hold on to, the idea of perfect divine order. Everything is always in perfect divine order and *you* are part of that divinity. You literally come from God and you literally are spirit in a body. Your spirit does not always stay *in* your body, as I have discussed in my previous books, however, you are more spirit than you realize and you are becoming *aware* of the fact that you are. Right now you totally relate to your human, mental side. Very soon you will begin to relate more and more to the spirit that resides within.

Once you begin to relate to, and with, the spirit you, you will begin the *shift* to using spirit to guide rather than using your fearful mind to guide you. Spirit will guide you to give out larger and larger doses of light energy, or what I like to call spiritual generosity. Once you have reached this phase and can "let go" of your hold on criticism and judgment, you will be on your way "up." You really do want to be kind, you simply don't know that you do. If you are operating from spirit, the message will be loud and clear. If you are still operating from your fearful mind the message will be loud and clear. There is no confusion between spiritual generosity and judgment.

You say you are simply calling it what it is, but are you? You will know the difference between naming something and judging something. Judgment carries its own damning energy. Simply naming something like, "Oh, that's a flower," does not. Naming something like, "That is so mean and prejudice," carries a much heavier energy. If you can't come to a neutral place in your feeling regarding your assessment, do not discuss the matter! Now I've done it! I am asking you to let go of political and social debate. Yes! I am. Is it really necessary for you to get all riled-up and *discuss* the state of affairs of the world? What does it do for *you*? What do *you* personally gain? I would like you to use your *power* wisely and raise *you* "up" not send you "down."

***

You will begin to see how to exist without concern for your future once you begin to live in the moment. Your energy is here and now. You do not exist in a future or a past. All time is this instant. You see time as linear with the line drawn back into your past and forward into your future. Time is instantaneous and it is all happening this moment. There is no past, there is no future. There is only the "now." This instant is the only time there is.

Your past is here and your present is here and your future is here. It is all here and it exists right now. You are a multi-dimensional being *existing* in many levels of reality at exactly the same moment.

So, what happens when you leave this life and move on to the next? You literally go to a new reality or enter a new dimension. You are a multi-dimensional being! So, once you move *on* to a new dimension, you continue to exist. Not only do you continue to exist, you continue to grow and to expand as God.

So, here you sit in your present moment and you are concerned about a future that is already *alive* in this exact moment. Everything has already occurred and you are simply becoming part of All That Is. As you become more and more *aware* of the part that you play, you will begin to calm down and watch the movie as it unfolds. No one really dies! No one ever ends. No one ever exists in just one dimension. There is no singular "I" there is only "all." You are "all" part of the same spiritual being, or force, or source and you are injecting yourself into different roles in order to *experience* that particular role. Play your role well. Love being in *your* personal role. You are beautiful, talented actors and you are *creating* a play within a play, and you do not realize how powerful *you* are at creating....

*Y*ou will begin to understand how you are multi-dimensional once you begin to open up to the possibilities of your life. There is so much more to you than you realize and the possibilities are limitless.

You are a limitless divine entity, and you are using so little of your potential right now that you *think* your human side is all that exists for you. You will begin to see how your divinity is part of your nature by *allowing* yourself to *act* as though you are divine. You spend most of your time acting like a frightened little child, who is trying to manipulate all the other children out of your fear and mistrust of life. This is your greatest hurdle. If I can just get you to see how fear and mistrust create more fear and mistrust, you will feel more confident in your life and you will begin to *allow* life to give to you in very big ways.

Fear and mistrust get you nowhere that you want to be. Fear and mistrust allow you to squeeze the life force out of you. You may think that you are being smart to look ahead with worry and concern; however, you are simply digging yourself into a hole. Once you see or become *aware* of your energy flow, you will understand the importance of acceptance and embracing life "as it is." The more you can *accept*, the greater your ability to *receive*.

Look at it this way. You are energy and life is energy. You may block energy by building walls of non-acceptance in order to protect yourself from what you think is bad energy. You build these walls of protection and you block out everything else. All the good energy is blocked also. You do not simply filter out the stuff *you* call bad, you filter out all energy! Your life becomes narrower and smaller, your mind becomes narrower and smaller and you are left with not much to look forward to. You begin to put a lot of energy into pushing at and bossing everyone else around, simply because you are not happy with your life! You do not like the view from where you stand, and I will tell you now that the view is being created by you and ruled by you, and you are the only one who can change your perspective and move you into a whole new reality.

Lift yourself "up" to a new perspective by dropping your walls of protection. "You need your walls to protect you," - you shout! No, you do not. You need freedom from the fears you are projecting out onto the movie screen of your life. You require love, not more fear. You require acceptance, not more judgment. You wish to rise up and to expand and take in more light/God-awareness. Take down your walls. They are blocking you from receiving. Allow life "in." Allow God energy "in." You are divine. You are not meant to hide in fear and blame life and others for everything that *you* are projecting.

Move yourself out of the hole you have put yourself in. Start small by *allowing* for the possibility that just one of the many things, that you *view* as awful, really has a divine purpose. There is no right or wrong here. There is only *your* perspective. Are you making yourself narrow minded and small or are you *allowing* for a broader perspective? Remember - you are a powerful creator and you are meant to be limitless.

*W*hen you begin to see how you *create* your world by deciding how to color every situation that comes up, you will be accepting yourself as well as your world. This will be due to the fact that you are now seeing from a whole new perspective or level of awareness.

Most of what you *decide* to color as dark and ominous is simply frightening to you. If you do not understand it and it frightens you, you then call it awful, or horrific, or just disgusting. Most often the situations that are judged by you to be awful, or unacceptable, are simply out of your field of acceptance and likability. You all have your likes and your dislikes, and you all have your limits on what you will *accept*. Some of you are extremely negative and very limited in what you see as good or okay. Others are more open-minded and a bit more liberal in their views of life and the world. This allows you to be a little more flexible and free with your thoughts and beliefs; however, you may end up judging those who are more conservative thinking.

Those who are more conservative will have a greater tendency to not change and not *allow* for change. It is good to change, and to move your energy in an upward direction at this time if you wish to gain pleasure and joy of life. If you are happy and joyful where you are, it is good to stay where you are. If you can find peace and happiness, with little or no frustration with your life and your world, you are ahead of the game. If, however, you are uncomfortable and afraid of the direction that you *believe* life is headed, you may wish to rethink your stance or your position on certain topics. If you can't see a situation as positive, do not dwell on it, "let it go." Allow all situations to be *beyond* your scope of understanding until you can move "up" to higher awareness.

Once you move up to higher awareness, you will be in a new position to see greater detail in all situations. Please do not continue to judge and please stop insisting that everyone see it your way. Your way is simply what you have settled for right now, and your way simply depends on *your* level of awareness and the amount of fear that you carry within you. Please do not try to talk others into fearing what you fear. I am trying to raise you "up" to a new reality which is quite a task, especially if you insist on seeing the worst in life.

Let it go! Come on "up" to the light....

As you continue to grow in awareness and illumination, you will begin to rise up to a whole new dimension. This dimension will *allow* you to receive the gifts that are already alive and in existence in this higher dimension. This level of reality is one of great movement and the ability to take on light. The more light you take on, the higher you rise. The higher you rise, the more gratitude you give off. The more gratitude you give off, the better you feel. The better you feel, the more love (acceptance) you give. The more love you give, the more love (acceptance) you receive.

It's all there within you. The power to raise your self up is right inside of you. You may continue to sit around and bemoan the circumstances of your life, or you may use your power to *create* a whole new view of life. You will find that the easiest way to access a new reality is to let go of your judgments against your current reality. Judgment will hold you in place and create a negative charge, or field of energy around you. Remember - you are energy and you are surrounded by energy.

You literally affect this energy field that you live in by giving it instructions. You send out signals that say, "Yes! Life is good" and you get more of what you send out. You control it all.

Now, here is the problem with you being in an unconscious state: you are totally unaware of the memories and beliefs that make you up. You require a draining of the trenches so to speak. You require a "letting go" in a very big way. You require a change of mind.

Now - don't get me wrong here and assume that God only wants you to change and be good. This is not what I am saying. What I am saying is that to get to what *you* want, you do require a change. You may stay where you are in your current reality and it is acceptable and even lovable to God. God has no vested interest in which direction you take in life. You are all actors in a play and you are making it up as you go. If you were children in a sandbox playing cops and robbers, God would not judge you as wrong. You are simply acting out roles in your imaginary world with other actors who have agreed to enter this imaginary world to take part in your little game.

You are not so bad as you think, you are simply confused and frustrated, and asking to be saved from this state of pain and confusion. I am answering that call for help and allowing you to see life in a new way. This is in an effort to assist those who wish to see a higher perspective. If you wish to see a higher perspective, you require change. If you are happy playing the part you are now in, continue as you have been. You are not doing anything wrong, you are simply *creating*. You are all creating and you are all gods. Do not give up on you, you are going to become the greatest you can be or you are going to remain where you are. This choice is yours and has always been yours. There is no wrong way to live your life. This applies to your neighbor also.

"Live and let live" and you will be moving in a whole new direction. If you wish to stay where you are, you may. Do not be afraid to change and do not be afraid to not change. If you decide not to change, you get to stay where you are. If you decide to change, you get to move on in a very big way.

Part of what we are doing here, is teaching you that you have the *choice* in all matters. You have the *power* within you to move up or down and even sideways if you like. You may decide to ignore all this information and go a whole new direction. God does not judge you no matter where you go or what you do. God *sees* the sandbox you are in and God simply watches his children (parts of himself) as they play in the field of creative possibilities.

You are each going to make a decision to rise up at some point, only because you will grow out of this game as you take on more and more awareness. After all, even children grow up and grow tired of playing make-believe in their sandbox. Even children move on and change how they see the world. You will grow and you will see everything differently in time. For now you will continue to entertain yourself with this game of make-believe, and you will continue to believe in good guys and bad guys. For now you are enjoying your ability to create in an entertaining way.

When you decide this is no longer fun, you will change your ways and you will begin to wish for something a little less frustrating and a little more peaceful. This is when you tune in to the energies of love and acceptance. This is when you begin to grow in a whole new direction. This is when you move up into a new perspective, one that *allows* for peace on earth and love of all….

༄༅

*Y*ou are beginning a new phase in your evolution as a species. You are at the precipice of a whole new way of viewing being human. It will no longer be considered important to do more in order to achieve more. It is going to become important to simply "be" and to become "aware."

Awareness is the new goal in this new millennium. Awareness is the gateway to receiving the benefits and the gifts of life. This world that you live in *appears* three-dimensional to you now, however, this is all about to change. You have been moving for some time now into a more fourth and fifth dimensional way of viewing life. Once you are in the fifth dimension, love (acceptance) will come easily to you and you will feel good more often than not.

So, as you continue to change your perception in an effort to gain a higher perspective, I wish you to remember that you are God. You are divine in nature and you are here to enjoy this experience of expansion. You may choose to see life as a school with lessons to be learned, however, that is simply one out of many ways of viewing your purpose in human form.

For the most part you are simply expressing as God. You may be, or do, or behave in any way that you choose. This is not a world of judgment and punishment unless *you* say that it is. If you *choose* to see it that way then that is what you get. Think of it as *ordering* what you want from a giant never-ending menu of possibilities. You get to choose where you go and what you see. It's all here already and it exists in this giant field of possibilities that you play in. Yes! This is all play and fun, and somehow you got it all twisted around and you turned your game of fun into misery and suffering.

So, how would you like to come out of misery and into joy? You will find it easier to live *in* joy than to exist in misery. First off you want to feel joy. So, I highly suggest that you lighten up and not be so serious. You are, after all, a "light" being. You are only human to house your "being." Begin to see yourself as a spirit living inside of a body instead of focusing totally on the body. You are body, mind and spirit. You use your body like you would use a car to run you around, and most of you take greater care of your cars then you do your bodies. You also abuse your mind with your own thoughts. Do you *realize* that your brain is literally *affected* by the thoughts that you dwell on daily? Fear and worry will damage the neurons in your brain. These neurons constantly connect and reconnect. A bad connection may cause big problems and affect the functions within the body. Please be kind to your brain by sending lighter, brighter thoughts through it.

You may think that you are a very good person and you may look down on others as being bad; however, your brain sends those signals through your body and "you" get to feel the effects of those judgmental thoughts. Your brain is affected and your life is affected. Look; I realize I am being repetitive here; however, repetition is what your brain requires in order to rewire and reconnect neurons in a whole new way. Once you get in the "habit" of seeing life differently, you will be closer to your goal. And just what is your goal? I would assume that you are reading a book titled "Your Individual Divinity," because you are on a spiritual path of enlightenment. When one is enlightened one becomes aware of their own divinity and their own ability to create.

Use your power wisely! Do not worry and fret that you will not do well. You are changing every day in every way, you simply are not "aware" that you are. Now you are becoming aware and you are "receiving" information that will assist you in your rise up. The more aware you become the higher you go. Remember - you exist in a field of energy that takes up all time and space. Everything has already been created and you are simply tuning in to the channel you wish to see. You live in a multi-dimensional universe and you are a multi-dimensional being. Shift your focus to the being in you, and you will begin to operate a little more from spirit and a little more from love.

Let go of your fears and your concerns. Hold on to your faith that life is good and fun and peaceful and generous and very, very accepting of you!

*Y*ou will become so much more of your own design by allowing yourself to simply flow with life. You are meant to be part of creation, and you are meant to rise to the top of this field that you exist in. You may choose to anchor yourself on the lower levels; however, you do have the capacity of rising all the way to the top. Of course, since this field that you exist in really has no top, or bottom, and is forever changing and growing, you are capable of forever changing and growing with it. The edges of infinity do not exist and the edges of you do not exist.

You are infinite by design and you are part of All That Is. So, if you are infinite and you are divine and you exist forever, don't you think it's time to relax and enjoy the ride? Everything is here to *serve* you and everything is at your disposal. You have been given this vast creation in which to play and create, and you do not yet realize your true nature, and you are not yet aware of your potential. Don't you think you should, or could, just let go and enjoy the ride? Please begin to see the gift in letting go and flowing with the rhythms of nature and life. Let go of fighting the flow and blocking energy.

So, as you let go, you may wish to look around you and begin to appreciate all that is being given to you. You have air to breathe, you have food available, you have flowers and trees for oxygen. You have the sun to grow your food supply and you have water to quench your thirst. There are those who do need help getting some of the basic needs of food and water, however, you are more than likely not one of them. Sometimes a soul, or many souls, will volunteer to come into this realm to show you how blessed you are, and how grand you are. These souls will often arrive in large groups just to get your attention. You see, you often work with other souls in your great movie, in order to create intrigue and diversity and depth of passion. You may even play this role from time to time yourself. All movies are designed by you and you only see what *you* have decided to see.

You will also see what you have decided is most entertaining for you, and sometimes you even see what is most educational for you. You are the designer of your personal role in this movie, and you usually design a life plan before you come in at birth. This, of course, is you the spirit/soul you, and you usually enter this earth with a plan or design. Often there is no design and you simply enter this world of illusion to enjoy it; however, if you came in with a plan, you will more than likely have set up situations that will assist you in your own personal experience. Some of you choose your parents and even your siblings. Some of you (soul you) decide ahead of time how to act out your role and who you will act with. Some of you (soul you) decide ahead of time how to best achieve the goals you choose for this particular lifetime.

Some of you (soul you) decide ahead of time if you will enter the fetus at birth, or after birth. Some of you (soul you) decide not to enter earth and to move on to other dimensions and playgrounds. Some of you (soul you) actually stay with the God force and observe the show you put on. So, who are you? Who is your neighbor, and who says you know best, and that you have all the information you require to judge anything in this *created* reality?

Give it a rest. Let go of judgment and just flow with life, and watch, and observe, and do not get so attached to results. This is the key to happiness and to peace of mind. There is no need to get yourselves so riled-up about life on planet earth. You are right here inside of God and you cannot really die. You are part of me…. I am part of you. You will find that I take up all space and time and I always will. I am not going away from you, and you only *think* you have left me… you have not! You are here within All That Is and you are alive and well and loved and cared for.

Look around you! See the good! Look for the good! See the colors, the beautiful colors of your life. See the beauty in every day of life. Look for things you love and focus on them every day. This will allow you to raise your attention in an upward direction. This will allow you to move in an upward direction. If you see everything as going down or going to hell, you will begin to go down. You move in the direction you focus on. Think of yourself as a vehicle that you can guide. Positive, uplifting thoughts will uplift or take you "up." Negative or down-putting thoughts will bring you down. It's all just energy and has nothing to do with right or wrong or good or bad. It's energy. You are energy. Bring yourself up to the higher realms by focusing on the higher thoughts.

Higher energy is simply lighter energy. Lighter energy weighs less or has less density. The lightness of your being is inside of you, and is there to guide you and assist you in this part you are playing. Access your light being, your soul, your spirit. Get to know this most important part of you. How? Go within to where the soul is housed. *You* are right there within you. You may continue to ignore this part of yourself, or you may connect with your spirit/soul and begin to merge with spirit in an effort to rise up in awareness and light.

Do not give up on you. You are the light and the life of your world. You are God incarnate and you are more powerful than you realize. If you choose to connect with your soul at this time, I would like to assist you. My pen (Liane) and I have written a series titled the *Loving Light Books Series*. This series will give you the basics of connecting with spirit in very simple terms. Do not judge the simplicity of this material, as it has been written in such a way that it enters the subconscious in an effort to bypass the more judgmental conscious part of your mind. This information will allow you to very gradually "open" up to receptivity of spirit, or God force. I do not say this lightly, as you are so afraid and mistrustful at this point in your evolution, that you do not *allow* God in.

♒〰♒

*T*he most important thing for you to remember, if you choose to raise your vibration, is love. Love is acceptance and love begins at home. Now, I realize that I told you at the beginning of this book that gratitude is your most important goal. I use gratitude to teach you, as love is a more difficult concept for you to grasp. Yes - love is the most complex of emotions. You might find love baffling and irritating and confusing and even painful. Love is really none of these; however, you have become so confused that you do not know how to love unconditionally.

Unconditional love is acceptance without attachment.

97

When you can *accept* your self or any other without being attached to their behavior, you are then encroaching on unconditional acceptance. Love is taking the time to realize that another person or animal or thing has value.

Once you begin to love unconditionally, you will see how energy can be accepted or rejected. When you reject energy, you push it away. When you accept energy, you are allowing it in.

Now, when you accept a person, this does not necessarily mean that you love this person romantically. For the most part romantic love is a pairing up or partnership. When romantic love dies the partnership is over, and very often your lives are left in pain and suffering. This is due to the fact that you only love and accept those you find attractive. You find them attractive because you want something from them. You may want love, you may want attention, you may want their wealth or you may want companionship. Either way, you are *expecting* them to fulfill a *need* that you have. You may be a rescuer, and decide that this person you have become attracted to needs you in some way. Either way, this attraction is not unconditional.

Many of you are also drawn together by your past wounds. You share certain painful experiences and so you are literally attracted to one another's pain. Remember - you are all energy and you attract to you that which is *in* you. So now we have you attracting what is in you and you call it love. I call it magnetism and attraction. So, we have magnetism and attraction all mixed in with love, and I come along and tell you that God is unconditional love and light and well, you see how the meaning of what love and light are can get a little distorted.

I would like to see you learn to love your self unconditionally in order to draw the energy of unconditional love to you. It all begins and ends with you. You create everything you see and I would love for you to see love. Gratitude is your doorway to love. Be as grateful as you can for your self and for every little thing in your life. Show gratitude whenever and wherever possible. Gratitude will eventually lead to love, and self-love will eventually lead to love of all.

So, love you unconditionally in order to love all unconditionally. Your barometer is you. How much love do you carry *within* you? Your love is reflected out onto the viewing screen of your life. If you see love everywhere you look, you are getting there. Where is there? There is light. You are becoming lighter and lighter, and you will soon achieve liftoff and lift "up" to the next dimension. So focus on gratitude, which will move you into appreciation, which will soon lead to total unconditional acceptance. Total unconditional acceptance is love, and love will *open* you up to *receive* big time. You will be raising yourself up to a whole new wave or stream of reality. You will be lifting yourself up to the next dimension or a parallel reality to your own.

Do you feel it coming at times? Do you have moments of great joy and contentment? Those moments are short breakthroughs to the next dimension. You may access any reality you choose. Once you are in a state of high vibration you automatically draw closer to a high vibrating parallel reality. You may enter for a brief time and *receive* all that is there, or you may decide you enjoy it so much that you decide to stay.

❧

*A*s you grow in awareness you become more of what you truly are. You are a light being with infinite wisdom and you are in a situation that allows you to deny your true nature.

As you move towards awareness and out of denial, you will become very happy to know *you*. You are so dense at this time that you do not see a majority of what exists all around you. You are totally and completely unaware of circumstances, and even events, that occur right within your personal reality. You have learned to blind yourself to the truth in an effort to gain ground in this material plane. You required a denseness in order to match the vibration of matter. Now that you are *in* matter, it is time for the next phase.

This next phase is ascension. You will begin to raise your self up out of the denseness of the material world and you will do so by your vibration. The higher you go, the lighter you feel. The lighter you feel, the better you feel. The better you feel, the happier you become. The happier you become, the more loving you will be. Joy begets more joy, and soon you will be living in the light of love and joy and bliss.

So, this is your future! You are headed "up" and out of the denseness and confusion that has been your home. The most difficult part is getting you to move. You hate change and you are *attached* to this material plane that you entered. As you begin to let go in little ways, you will begin to feel unsafe. You feel safe when you are holding on tight, and I am asking you to let go and float. It is most difficult for many of you to let go in this way. You are attached to so many things and ideas and ways of doing things that you do not feel safe when these things are taken from you.

To rise up you must first "let go." It is not an easy task for you, and you will find yourself missing your old ways and your old attachments. Society teaches you to be a certain way, and you want so badly to be loved, and to fit in, that you may have to wait until a majority of the population *decides* to change. Once they all *decide* it is okay to accept a different way of being, you may feel more comfortable changing who you think you are.

It is most difficult at this time to get you to be different than your contemporaries. You do not like to feel different and you do not like to be made fun of or bullied. Bullying is one way to keep people in line and performing in a specific manner. Another way to bring people under control is to use fear tactics. "If you don't do it this way you go to hell" - this is a fear threat. When you are held in check by fear, you do not explore and you do not expand. In order to rise up, you must be willing to expand, and you must be willing to be different, and you must be willing to change.

When you first entered this dimension, you did so with a goal in mind. That goal was to impregnate matter with your beingness, and to take on matter to the extent that you literally become one with it. The next step is to raise the vibration of matter in an effort to *see through the illusion.* So now we have you immersed in the lower, slower vibrations of matter and it is now time to raise your vibration back up to your normal mode. Your normal mode of vibrating is quite high due to the fact that you are a light being.

You have been lost in matter for some time now. God is finally stepping in to say, "Okay, it's time to come home now." You are in your grand movie, and you are afraid to leave the role that you are playing simply because you don't *know* who you really are.

You are not so much human as you are God energy. You are not so much matter as you are pure energy. You are not so much fear as you are love. You are not so much darkness as you are light. It is time now to wake up and know the truth. It is time now to move forward to this next step in evolution. Some of you feel this strongly. Some of you do not feel like you fit in on earth. Some of you *know* that you belong elsewhere. Some of you know that there is much more than this small dimension. Some of you know that you are meant to be something greater, and you are reaching out to spirit to guide you. Some of you know that God is somehow part of you, and some of you know that you are on the precipice of something big.

This is a great time of change and the changes you see are for the better. Please continue to look upon life with kindness and gratitude. This will allow you to raise your vibration gently and gradually. You will lift your self up and you will lift your personal reality up. This will continue until each individual entity has risen to a state of awareness that allows for you to *see* who you truly are, and to *know* your own divinity.

You are God and you are becoming *aware* of this truth.

❧

*Y*ou will soon learn how you destroy your own creative energy by not *allowing* your energy to flow freely. Sometimes you stop yourself from being the best version of yourself, out of a need for self-control. You have lost your natural trust and your ability to reach out and support others.

Most of you have had experiences early on that have left you in a non-trusting state of mind. You find it difficult to trust others, and so you put your guard up and your armor on. I would like to see you lower your guard and become vulnerable. You will find that vulnerability is a place that is very uncomfortable for you.

You do not enjoy feeling vulnerable because it leaves you feeling *open* and exposed. You want to receive the gifts and joys of life, and yet you remain *closed* and guarded. I would highly suggest that you begin to *open* in an effort to *receive.* You may choose to remain closed and guarded; however, you will not be moving in the direction you hoped for, which is "up" to the next level of energy.

Please stay as open and receptive as possible. Please be more childlike and less adult like. Adults in your society are *trained* and *taught* to let go of fun and silliness. Adults are told to grow up and behave. Adults are taught the fine art of manipulation and control. Adults are led to believe that they are better off to hide who they are, and *act* as though they are more sophisticated than they feel. Adults are trained to behave as though they respect life when, in actuality, they do not (for the most part) understand life.

As children, many of you put on airs and pretended to

be adults in your make-believe games. This is how many of you behave to this day. You are so out of touch with who you are that you are *pretending* to be the person you think you should be. I would like to see you reconnect with your inner self and begin to know your true self. If you feel like you do not fit in, it is more than likely because you are not being your true self.

So, how do you get to a place of acceptance and love of self? You first *open* up to your inner self. Have you heard the saying, "All your answers are within?" This saying is quite true and you will become aware of feelings and thoughts and beliefs that you carry "within" you, which are directly affecting the energy of your life. You require self-knowledge and self-awareness. You require an open mind and an open heart. Many of you have wounds that you carry, and memories surrounding those wounds that require healing and letting go. It is good to know who you are, and it is good to explore your own emotions and to allow any guilt and blame that you carry to come to the surface and be released. Guilt and blame create anger and frustration and, eventually, self-punishment. Self-punishment is often in the form of loss.

When you were very young, how were you punished for doing wrong? Were you yelled at, or were you hit, or were you punished by losing something like your music or television privileges? Were you kept home from going out and playing with the other children? However you were punished is more than likely how you punish *you.* You have a big event coming up and all of a sudden *you* give yourself a cold and cannot go to this event. If you were hit and physically punished, *you* will punish yourself by falling, or twisting an ankle, or hitting your thumb as you try to hit a nail. How many of you have a running dialogue in your head where you call either yourself or someone close stupid, lazy or incompetent? This could be how you were punished as a child.

All punishment is *learned* punishment and it is part of the training process of turning a child into a respectful adult. Now, I do *not* condone the use of pain in any way and I do *not* judge the use of pain. Remember - everything is energy and *you* are energy. With energy there is cause and effect. If energy moves in one direction, there will be an effect. If energy moves in an opposite direction, there will be an opposite effect. So, I suggest you begin to look within and observe your self and turn your energy around. If you are one who punishes by yelling and getting angry, you may change this behavior by looking at why you are so upset and hurt. Are you carrying huge amounts of blocked energy that causes your outbursts? If you are constantly judging others, I wish you to look at any guilt you might carry. If you carry big guilt energy, you will be very sensitive to any criticism and you will more than likely find yourself getting sick at some point. "Guilt" is a decree handed down by a judge that then doles out your punishment. People who carry heavy guilt energy are often sick a lot.

If, on the other hand, you were often punished by losing your privileges or use of toys, you will more than likely punish your self by taking away things. You buy a new car and soon after you accidentally dent it, or you buy a new computer and right away you get a virus or it crashes. You may take away events as well. You may be the one who is left out or disinvited to a party. Most adults who were punished by loss techniques grow up using this technique on their own children, and it is still taught as a good practice to this day.

I will remind you once again that *it's all energy, people!* Cause and effect is what you are dealing with. Energy *held* within the body creates for you, as well as new energy that you send out every single day. So, let go of all that is not serving you. Go *within* and begin to heal *you.* You want quick fixes and instant gratification, and I will tell you now that you were trained and programmed to be a certain way, and you can untrain and reprogram your self to be any way you would like to be.

You are the one in charge. You may continue to remain *closed* down or you may *decide* to *open* up. If you decide to open up and go within, you will find many books and recordings to assist you. You may even enjoy those listed at the back of this book. For now, I will simply ask that *you* consider creating a new, *open* version of you. This will allow you to begin to *receive* a great deal that you have been blocking.

When it comes to anger, you are easily triggered. Most of you lose your cool the minute something does not go your way. You get upset and frustrated with those around you simply because you are uncertain of your own beingness. You are uncertain that this other person may degrade, or punish you, or disrespect you in some way.

Often you will find that you even get angry at life and

at situations in life. You are becoming an angry and frustrated race of beings. You do not know how to flow with life; you only know how to criticize life. When you criticize life, you are basically calling it bad or wrong. You are basically *blaming* life for your problems. When you blame life, or another individual, for your problems you are making yourself a victim. If you would like to no longer *feel* like a victim I would suggest that you begin to control your angry thoughts.

Allow yourself to be at peace by allowing yourself to skip the drama of anger. Anger is a way of getting your needs met, and anger at another does not hurt them so much as it damages the connected neurons in your own brain. Not only does anger damage parts of the brain, fear also has this effect on the brain. Now, when you become very angry, you create large waves of energy that *move* out from you and push everything away. Anger is such a strong energy that people *feel* your angry energy and move away from you. Not only do people move away, animals may move away, and your energy field surrounding you becomes very dense. This energy field is then lowering you due to its denseness. You will then find yourself in a lower vibrating stream of energy or reality. Raise yourself "up" by seeing your situation differently. Stop looking for the worst and you will begin to see the best.

You are always looking for problems so you can nip them in the bud before they spread. I will tell you now that energy *flows* in *waves*. Waves go up and they go down. *Accept* the flow and let go of your *need* to create drama around any situation. *Allow* life to unfold and you will be *accepting* - you will be accepting all the gifts that come in on the wave of energy that is your personal reality. Anger will send you to the lower vibrations, and *if* you choose to rise "up" to the higher vibrating realities, you will wish to switch off your *choice* to use anger.

"You can't help it if someone angers you" - you shout! Yes. You can. You *decide* which emotions to use in any given situation. Most of these choices have been programmed into you and may be unprogrammed or reprogrammed at any time. A child grows up emulating the adults around them. You are taught and trained by your parents and by society. You may now choose to *grow* beyond this training by letting the old programming go. Here's a little trick I taught Liane. You may catch yourself when you have a negative thought and you may rub your thumb on your middle finger and say, "Oh no you don't, you come right back here." This will not only make you more aware of your negativity, it will also retract the negative energy that you send out from you on a daily basis.

Now, I have told you before that I spent ten years working with Liane to write a series of books to guide you each "within" to your own God self. In these books you will find many techniques on how to handle many life situations, and on your emotional body and how to heal it. If you are interested in really moving into ascension, you will find this series of twenty books most helpful. This has been a lifetime of work for my pen (Liane) and she has overcome her anger and her pain from childhood abuse. The information I have channeled *through* her has had a very positive effect on her emotional body, and this in turn has raised her mental and physical bodies "up" from where they once were.

Do not be afraid to change and to confront your own personal fears. Do not be afraid to go *within* you and see what makes you tick. You are the cause of how energy moves to you. Change you and you change how energy moves to you.

⚜

*Y*ou have become human in an effort to experience the human condition. You found that you could change from spirit to matter and back again. This excited you and you began to play this little game for fun and for experience.

Now you are *in* matter and you have forgotten your original *intent.* Your original intention is to go and return. You go to the three-dimensional world of illusion and then you return to the God force or the field of All That Is. Once you have returned you automatically begin to remember who you are and how you originally left.

In the beginning you did not access your inner awareness because you thought it would take away the fun. After all, if you are going to play a game, you require some blocks to keep you stumped and block your easily winning. So, your blocks became important in this game of hide God from God. You began to go unconscious to the fact that you are indeed God, and you began to lose your awareness of your own spirit essence. Your own divinity became unknown to you in an effort to be more human. You might think of it as a game where you put on a costume and forget to take it off. You wear your costume for so long that you begin to *believe* that you are actually the princess, or the pirate, that you originally portrayed.

You are not this role that you now play. You are divine

in nature and you are hiding in this material plane of illusion. You are not so much human as you are God. You are part of this divine energy that makes up God, and you have gone unconscious to the fact that you are. So now God is injecting energy into this plane of illusion, a little at a time, to let you know who you are and to raise you back "up" so that you might return to All That Is, as was your original intent. So far, many are responding at this time, and many of you are beginning to realize that you are much more powerful than you now believe.

Many of you are beginning to communicate with spirit and to understand that life has many layers other than those you see. Please be *open* and *accepting* of the paranormal experiences that are beginning to occur on earth. You are simply being shown that you are so much *more* than you currently *believe* you are. If you can *allow* for the expansion of human thought, you will be adding to the *awareness* of this world that you currently live in. You are not meant to fear every new idea that comes along. You are meant to grow and expand the spiritual essence that you carry, until it literally raises you "up" out of this dimension to the next dimension.

You cannot raise up when you are being held down by fear. You cannot claim your divinity if you do not *accept* paranormal activity. Paranormal activity is not normal activity. It is called paranormal for a reason. Stop believing that you have all the answers. You do not; if you did you would not be sitting here reading this book. You would be back home in the God force.

So, how does God get you to come home and wake up? First we begin to feed you information that will allow you to see yourself differently. Then we begin to reprogram you so that you become *aware* of your true nature. Next we begin to send in help in the way of very enlightened beings who retain a great deal of their awareness. These beings become your spiritual teachers and allow you to see God without the fear of God. Once you no longer fear God, you may then *accept* your self as part of God.

So we now have you preparing to wake up to the fact that you are a spirit in human form, and we can now begin to guide you home. Once you become aware of the *spirit in you*, you will begin to listen for guidance. Sometimes this guidance is literally a voice, other times it comes as a feeling. Either way, you begin to be guided, and you end up devouring books and films that raise your awareness and answer your questions. This is how we will guide you home to your source.

You are not in this alone! There are many who have returned from your experience, and there are many who continue to enter the earth game in an effort to one day guide you home. Some of you will not wake up until you have experienced a few more lifetimes. This too is okay. Everything is actually okay and in divine order.

So, if you are feeling guided, trust your guidance. If you are feeling that you know all the answers, I suggest you continue to go *within* your own self and attach to the spirit *within* your own body. You may even have a good conversation with God as others are now doing. Of course, you will wish to be careful as to whom you tell. It is not yet fashionable to *receive* answers from God. It is okay to speak to God, but to *receive* information from God is considered blasphemy. So, if you begin a dialogue you will wish to know that you are not alone in your communication with God; you are simply on the cutting edge of something fairly new. This little technique will catch on, and when it does it will become very popular. For now, you may start by consciously connecting with the spirit *in* you, and you will be guided to a direct connection to God. After all, God *is* you and you *are* God....

꧁꧂

*F*rom the time you first began to play in the material plane of matter, you have been working on figuring out just what to do. You always are on a quest to discover more about the atom and the subsequent particles that make up the atom.

You spend much of your time working on discovering how you live as a sentient being, and on what makes some of you different than others. Most of you are so caught up in daily life that you simply want to be accepted and loved, and even admired for the roles that you play in the lives of others. Then we have those who question, and wonder, and *feel* like there is something more than simply fitting into society as a whole. The ones who fit in, and have an abundance of love and nurturing, seem to be happy and do well with this earth experience. Those who do not understand how to fit in and follow the rules of society, have a much more difficult time.

As far as you are concerned, you are happy (for the most part) if you have love and some wealth. What if wealth was not an issue and you had all the money you could ever want? Would you still feel the *need* to improve yourself and to improve your life? Is financial abundance a big gift or is it a detriment that causes greater problems in your life?

Today we will discuss wealth and how it may lift you up or bring you down....

For the most part great wealth can be a wonderful gift. It will buy you the nice home and automobile and even a plane you might *desire*. Then you may use your wealth to assist others who are in need. We also have those who use their wealth to block others. You see this often in corporate wars and in politics. So, you have your wealth and you decide that you know best who should be in power politically, and so you use your money to block your opponent from winning the political race. You might say that you put your money where your mouth is. You put financial power behind your words. Money is now being *used* as a weapon.

You may also withhold your financial support and *use* your money as a bargaining tool. Either way, money is being *used* to control others. So, money has now become not only a weapon, but also a *tool* to manipulate and control. So, how do you *use* your money? Do you *use* it to punish and to reward? Many of you use wealth (no matter the amount) to manipulate and control life. You feel that money is power, and sometimes you feel that you could have so much more *power* if you just had more money. Power is not derived from control. If you *use* your finances to gain control and respect, you are missing the boat and you are in for a rude awakening at some point in your evolution and your understanding of wealth.

Money, as all in this created environment, holds the energy of the meaning that you give to it. You must come to a place of financial wisdom if you seek *balance* in this material world that you now inhabit. Use your money as you would use your thoughts. The higher the vibration of the intent for your wealth, the higher your money can take you. Remember, money is not vulgar! Money, as everything in this material world, has the meaning that you personally give it. If you say it is vulgar then you are creating it as such in your own personal reality. If you say that rich people are greedy and vulgar, then that is the belief that you are forming within your personal reality. If you believe something to be bad on some level, you will not wish to draw it to you. As a matter of fact, you will more than likely block it from becoming a *gift* in your life.

Be very careful how *you* create your personal reality. Send out only the most positive energy waves. This will draw you into a personal reality that is filled with positive energy regarding all topics and aspects of life on this material plane. Use your thoughts wisely and use your emotions wisely. Stop throwing your weight around as though you are a tough guy. Be soft and kind and gentle and you will draw yourself into a soft, kind, gentle world. Do not despair, you are all rising up (some slower than others) and you are all learning how to use energy wisely. When it comes to personal wealth it is best to not *use* your money to control others. Instead you might choose to use your money to lift others up! This will affect *you* in a very big way, as you will be lifting *you* up!

As you continue to grow in awareness, you will continue to rise up in joy and gratitude. The higher you rise, the greater your love of life will become. If you do not appreciate life, you will more than likely stay where you are. The key to appreciation is acceptance. Acceptance is the ability to flow within any stream of energy or any situation. Always remember that everything is simply energy in movement, and the one thing constant about energy is that it is *always* moving and changing.

So, if you wish to stay the same, you must continue to stay put and not move with the energy. If you wish to move up, then I suggest you let go of your *hold* on your way of doing things and *allow* life to unfold around you. I am not asking you to accept punishment by another, nor am I asking you to allow yourselves to be used by others. I am simply stating here that there may be a better way of dealing with life than to always try to control and manipulate everyone to be more like you.

You seem to think that you are only safe if everyone else behaves as you behave. Many of you are angry beyond words and you are ready to explode. This is why you have social and political uprise. You are so upset that you no longer criticize with just words. You now speak with your might and with your weapons. I would ask that you put down your weapons and heal your anger before you hurt someone or yourselves.

As you continue to raise your level of awareness, you will begin to see how *you* may be causing some of your own problems. The best way to let go of anger is to go to the source of anger. Most of you become angry because you are not getting what you want! On a spiritually *aware* scale you

115

are like a two-year-old throwing a tantrum. You have totally lost your ability to hear (listen) and you are simply spouting off *your* personal beliefs and ideals.

Please begin to see how you are stirring the energy and causing waves that swamp your own boat. Please begin to understand that you are part of God, and *you* create the life and the world that you see. Please begin to choose to express love instead of fear. Please begin to allow love to grow inside of you. You are affecting *you* in a very big way by using *your* anger as a tool to create your personal reality. Please let go of your hold on anger and judgment and criticism. Please begin to see the promise in using love (acceptance) as your tool for creation. You can all afford to be a little more loving and a little less critical.

The changes that come within your body and your mind, when you run the energy of love and gratitude through the cells within you, are extreme compared to the changes from constantly running fear and anger and judgment through your cells. You will lift you "up" in many ways. Your health will improve in many ways, and your ability to feel at peace with life will be your biggest reward. Right now so many of you are at odds with life, and as explained earlier in this book *you* are your life.

So, let go of your need to be at odds with your life, or you!

❧

*Y*ou will soon discover your ability to forgive. You

will wish to forgive not only yourself, but *everyone* you have ever harbored dense energy feelings against.

Forgiveness is not actually taking on the energy, it is letting go of energy. When you forgive, you do not necessarily condone an act, you do however *release* the judgment placed on the act. Say you were accosted and beat up and left for dead. You hate the person who defiled you and disrespected you and maimed you for life. So now you have this disability from this particular incident and your life has been changed forever.

I do not wish for you to hurt yourself further by holding on to judgment. The dense energy of judgment will bring you down and your energy will suffer. You are made up of energy so this means that you will suffer. The fastest way to heal and to move forward is to let go of any judgment you might carry. Let it go and move on to the next phase of your life. This does not mean that you do not call the police, and it does not mean that you do not press charges and see your abuser stand trial for what he or she did. This does mean that you let go of any dense energy you might carry regarding this event.

Do not hate this abuser and do not *fear* this abuser. I know that this is a lot to ask, however, I also *know* that *you* are God and God does not judge anyone or anything. God simply *observes* all of creation with the clear awareness and insight that absolutely everything is an illusion, a drama, a play on a stage. None of this is what you *think* it is, and most encounters have been set up by you (spirit you) before you went on stage to act out your role.

So, if you are a victim I will suggest that you turn the other cheek and walk away, *knowing* that you will only bring you down, energy wise, by *seeking* to bring another down. I have given many scenarios in my *Loving Light Books Series* on everything from sexual abuse to killing. If you wish more insight on how to see specific situations differently you may wish to start there.

Now, for those who find this form of letting go and forgiving unattainable at this time, I would suggest that you seek professional help, so that you might have greater understanding of the psychology of pain and guilt and judgment. With professional help, you may be able to let go of some of the denser energies before the weight of them pulls you down further. Your goal is to go "up" not down. If you truly wished to go down, you would not have been guided to read this information.

As you continue to see how energy works, you will become more and more *aware* of how your life is simply a flow of energy. You get to *direct* the flow by how you see and *interpret* life. Say you are the victim of the attack we just spoke about. You are being beaten and abused. You may get up, dust yourself off and go on your way *knowing* that a very intense ball of energy just hit you, or you may go on and on about how hurt, beat and disrespected you have become. Remember - everything is simply energy.

So, you are feeling hurt and disrespected and in physical pain. Life is a series of ups and downs. You do not know how you ended up on the ground being beaten. You know that you have lived before in past lives, and you do realize that you may have built up enough harmful energy from a past life, that the energy of that life is just now surfacing *in* you in order to leave you. Why? Simply because *you* have *decided* to heal body, mind and spirit. You have *decided* to raise your self up to a higher dimension, and this causes any dense energy *within* you to come to the surface and *release,* so that you might lighten your load and rise up.

Do you feel like you are a victim and do you feel like you are being beaten up by life? Maybe, just maybe, you beat up someone, or many someone's, on a battlefield in a past life, and you carry so much guilt regarding this encounter that you are now releasing it by allowing this guilt to surface. Guilt is energy. Guilt says, "I did something wrong, I must be punished." Voila`! We now have this you accepting, or *receiving*, the energy that has been stored *in you* from a past life experience. It is energy! Energy stays *in* you if *you* hold on to it. Energy flows through you to release if you allow it to. The longer you hold it down in you, the longer *you* stay down. Why? Because you are energy! You are spirit/God/light energy and when you convert light into darkness you see and *feel* a denser, heavier energy.

Lighten you up! Lift you up! You can do this. You know how to let go and not get involved in the drama and conflict. All that you see is but a reflection of what is *in* you. Let go and see peace. Do not seek revenge on your self by seeking revenge on another....

❧

*T*he most difficult part of being human is dealing with pain. You have emotional pain as well as physical pain. I come along and tell you how everything is an illusion and you *know* that it is real because you can *feel* it. Here is the secret about pain. Pain is a signal that is being sent through your body to tell it that something is wrong. If you were to have certain parts of your brain removed completely, you would no longer *feel* any pain whatsoever.

There is a disease that occurs in some small children where they do not *feel* the sensation of pain. They could jump off the roof of a house and break every bone they have, yet not feel it. These children must be closely supervised at all times. Sometimes you find a patient who feels pain all the time but there is no reason for their pain. It is considered to be psychosomatic in nature.

So, if pain can be psychosomatic or totally absent in some, is it real? Is pain real or is it part of this illusion? Pain begins in your nervous center and moves out from your brain to tell you that you have a problem. Maybe you just twisted your ankle or banged your thumb with a hammer. Pain will signal you to get off your feet or to stop hitting your thumb. Severe pain can be debilitating and can cause you to be laid up for some time.

As you heal a wound, where does the pain go? As you heal, the pain signal stops. Sometimes the pain signal is triggered after many years and you now have an old wound, or war injury, or sports injury that begins to hurt. These are all ways that your body speaks to you. Your body is constantly communicating with you to let you know what is going on. Why? Because your body is made up of energy as well as mass, and your body communicates through a pattern of signals sent from the brain. This is why you can interrupt a pain signal by taking a pain pill.

Now is when it gets tricky. You take your pain pills and you take your pain medicine and you block the signals that your brain is sending to you. You literally shut off a warning signal coming from your body to tell your mind that you have a problem. Please begin to listen to your body. When your body says, "I'm full and don't require the whole pizza, or the full gallon of ice cream," do you listen or are you trying to shut your body up so you don't have to listen to it?

When your body says, "I had enough to drink and I am getting dizzy from this alcohol," do you listen or do you continue to bombard it with wine or liquor? When your body becomes sick from overindulgence in drugs, do you stop or do you try to anesthetize it further? Do you push your body to its limits with physical exercise just to win at sports and make millions, or do you find balance in all that you do? Do you shovel down your meals or do you eat slowly and *allow* your body to digest your food as you go? Do you even give your body a thought other than to look at it in disgust, in your mirror, for being too big or too fat or too wrinkled? Do you love your body and appreciate your body and thank your body every day for walking for you, and lifting for you, and breathing for you, and seeing for you; or do you simply *judge* your body for not walking well enough, or far enough, or fast enough? Do you love your body and thank your body, or do you simply wake up and drink a stimulant to make it go faster and do more?

Your body is a gift that is allowing spirit to play in matter. Wouldn't you like to thank your body and let go of all the judgments you hold against it? Don't you think you would be in a great deal of pain if you were ignored and pushed to do more every day like a slave? Wouldn't you give up and break down if you were so physically abused with medication and drugs and food and alcohol? Wouldn't you eventually just quit on your master?

Love your body! Appreciate your body! You live inside this vessel. Take good care of your body and it will serve you well....

❦

As you continue to grow in awareness, you will continue to expand in consciousness. Consciousness is the goal for those who are unconscious and beginning to wake up.

As you wake up, you will feel different. You will feel as though you have new insights regarding life and your role in life. You will begin to see life as less of a struggle and more of an adventure. Life will become more of a gift and less of a challenge.

Once you become conscious you will look at God in a new way. You will see how God is more than you ever dreamed. You will become *aware* of your connection to God, and you will let go of any fear regarding a judgmental, authoritative, punitive God. You will begin to understand the role that you are playing, and you will begin to play with the energy that is you and that you are a part of. Life will become a breeze and your anger at self and at life will fade away.

You are truly headed for heaven on earth once you wake up to the fact that you are creating your experience by your *reaction* to your *perceptions*. You see, everything is perception and nothing is real. You may continue to see life as difficult or you may *decide* that it's a beautiful life full of love and kindness. You get to *decide* each and every day whether you will see beauty and love or ugliness and fear.

You are in the power position and you have always been. You are free to decide what colors to paint and even how beautiful your personal painting will be. You are at the beginning stages in your ability to open up and *receive* the gifts that are here, right in front of you. Do not be afraid to look for the good in absolutely everything you see. Do not be afraid to see behind the illusion to the perfection of creation. Do not live *in* your fear. Your fear will only blind you to the beauty that is constantly available to you.

As you continue to wake up, you will discover things about yourself, and how *you* have been controlling and manipulating your life in an effort to *protect* yourself from all that you fear. If you can just let go and trust that life is good and you are good, you will be putting yourself in a very good position to rise "up" and feel even better about your personal reality.

It is all really a game and you are all becoming too serious and very stuck in your roles. Let go of your *need* to show off your riches and let go of your *need* to be "better than." You are all the same, and to be "better than" is no different than to be "less than." When you put someone above yourself you create separation. When you put them above you, you are sending a signal through your body that says, "I am less than." You are all one and that one that you are is total consciousness. That one that you are is the light of this world and the source of All That Is. That one that you are is the totality of All That Is.

You are this entire field of energy focusing on one tiny lifetime. You are this giant seer of all things and All That Is, and you are focused for this moment on your life "here" and your thoughts "now." You are choosing to focus on this tiny part out of all the vastness that is being displayed before you. You may choose to focus on a new part and you may choose to move anywhere within this field that you exist in and are part of.

The field is limitless and you are limitless. You may decide to *see* whatever you choose to see. As you raise your level of awareness, your *perception* of what you are seeing will *shift* upward, and once that takes place your *focus* is now in a new position which will allow you more and more beauty. Remember - it's all perception, or translation, of what you *think* you see. Let the translation be good and you will move in that direction. It's not really good (or bad), but I must speak to you in your own terms in order to assist you in your rise "up" out of this illusion that you are playing in....

⚜

*Y*ou all began the same way. You all came from the energy that is God and you all live in God. How can any of you be "less than" or "greater than" another? It is not possible. You are *all* exactly the same. You each chose the role you are now playing and you wear the appropriate costume for your role. Basically you fell asleep or went unconscious to the fact that you are all the same, and now you judge one another based on the roles that you all play. You sometimes judge the costume without getting to know the soul, and which role they have chosen.

So, here we have you all choosing to see the worst in one another instead of focusing on the best. You try to find information that will take down those you do not agree with, and you try to dishonor and discredit those you do not like. This slides you lower down the layers of energy realities. This basically sends you to the basement or bottom floor of this giant mansion you are exploring. If you *choose* to see everyone as equal and acceptable, you *allow* yourself to be equal and acceptable.

Once you have traveled down to the basement, or lower levels, you must then raise your energy back "up" if you wish to return to the higher waves of energy. You may bring yourself back "up" by accepting everyone as part of you (part of the whole of God). Once you are able to accept everyone as part of you, you will no longer see them as lower on the human totem poll than yourself. If you see them as higher on the human totem pole, you are sending yourself lower.

So, it all seems quite simple, doesn't it? You go "up" by *allowing* everyone to be just as good and wonderful and bright and godlike as you are. Very simple... that's God's way... that's how energy works.

If you continue to see yourself as above others, you will continue to push yourself down by pushing them down. See them as you and you as part of them.

⚜

*T*he only reason you would ever have to argue is to

convince yourself that you are good and wonderful and absolutely lovable. Other than that there is no reason for argument.

You try and you try and you cannot seem to teach yourselves to live peacefully. You command, you demand and you reject on a daily basis. I would really like to see you learn a little discipline and let go of this pain that you carry. You walk around wounded and you push one another's buttons, and you all have your walls of protection so high that you judge one another, and you judge situations as dangerous when they often are not. You are simply so fearful that you are pushing at life and at the world. When you push life away, you get left with emptiness. This space (emptiness) that you *feel* is separation. You have separated yourself from God and now you are separating yourselves from one another.

The greater the separation, the less love and acceptance you will feel. This is due to the fact that you are pushing away life, and you are your life. You *are* the dreamer of your dream and you *are* the one who directly experiences all of your feelings of anger. Your body is your vessel, and you are contaminating your personal space with this dense energy of anger and fear.

Here is the truth about anger: anger is fear in motion. You are afraid and so you get angry with everyone else. You basically blame everyone for your fear, because your fear is big and dense and it causes *you* pain. The best way to experience your fear is to *allow* it to come to the surface and float away. If a small child is terrified of dark spaces, or monsters under his bed, it will help to show him the space under his bed so he can see that the monsters are in his mind.

You all have monsters in your mind and those of you who are rising "up" at this time will be allowed to see your fears, so that you might *realize* they are only in your mind. You *fear* what you believe *might* happen, which is a form of projection. Basically, you are *projecting* an image out onto the viewing screen of your life. This image is a fearful one. This image causes you to be defensive and angry. This image is the image you *believe* in. Let this image of danger and fear go. Begin to see a new image and project this new image out on the viewing screen of your life. If there is no fear, anger cannot exist! Anger is simply an extension of fear. Let your fears go and begin to trust life and trust yourself and trust God... the God *in* you....

꙰

*W*hen you become lighter, you will see how you have held yourself down by using certain choices and decisions. Your choices and decisions determine your direction, and your feelings push you in specific directions. Normally you would wish for choices that are going to lift you up and not put you down.

You may begin to raise your energy up by using your thoughts to direct your feelings. Look at a flower or tree or the sky, any view that is calming and peaceful to you. Begin to see this object or scene through the eyes of admiration. You may choose to focus on the colors or on the movement as clouds float by, and leaves gently sway in the wind. Now begin to see this object of your appreciation crumble and

127

disappear. This is what it is like to die. You see this object of admiration and appreciation and then it is gone. You then mourn the loss of this view that you once had. If you can tune *in* to this view once again you will re-experience your feelings of admiration and appreciation.

This is how life works, your view, your perception is crumbled up and lost to you. Now I would like you to go back and re-experience this appreciation you once had.

Do you remember lying on the grass as a child and looking up at the clouds and seeing images there? You are going to find images in your mind that will lift you up and assist you in raising your energy vibration. This should be fun and easy for you. Do not worry so much about how long you can hold this image. Just pull it up from memory and feel the feelings attached to it. You might feel in awe of the beauty you are taking in, or you might feel happy to find a face or a puppy in the cloud formations. Remember the first time you viewed the night sky full to brimming with stars? This is something majestic to behold and it raises your level of energy just to picture it.

Always stay focused on the things that are appealing to you, and you will gradually *shift* your focus from what you do not like and will not accept, to what you do like and will easily accept. When you stay focused on the things you love, your feelings of love run through every cell in your body. When you see through the eyes of love, you are using your power to raise you up and lift your own personal energy.

Try to feel good as often as possible. You have spent a great deal of time worrying about tomorrow (a time that does not exist except in your imagination). The way to bring yourself back from worry-filled tomorrow's is to focus on fun-filled today's. Live in the moment as often as possible and you will be putting your power and creative force to good use. You *are* the creator of your personal reality, and you may assist yourself by allowing you to live in the moment and by focusing on what is here and now. The sky is always here. Nature is always here. Life is always here. Find a feeling you like and begin to *use* it to raise you up out of your worry and upset feelings. I am not talking about despair and grief and sorrow. I am talking about your day to day worry and concern and distrust.

Look for the good and the beautiful until you see good and beautiful everywhere! This will allow you to keep yourself from going lower into the denser feelings that can pull you down. Do not fret and do not struggle with your emotions. If you don't feel good simply observe your feelings until you can get past the urge to "act out." If you do "act out" in a negative way I would suggest that you stay calm and sit down and shut up. Sometimes it's best not to add fuel to the fire, and often you are in no position to create from higher vibrations when you have acted out from lower vibrations. You can always bring yourself back up by staying calm and observing a situation, rather than getting all involved with the energy and stirring things up more. Stay calm and breathe in and breathe out. Look for something you enjoy and appreciate, and focus on that until you are happy and feeling good. This brings your energy back into balance and will keep you from sliding down in an energy spiral.

Okay, this entire writing is a little subliminal and this is intentional. The intention here is to feed you information on a conscious level that you will *accept* and *allow* through to your subconscious. You may assist yourself with feelings and images and what you choose to focus on. You may also cause problems for yourself with feelings and images and what you choose to focus on.

So, for today I would like you to find something you enjoy looking at, and hold it in memory if you're going to be moving away from it at any time during your day. If you begin to fret or worry, or project your energy into an illusionary tomorrow filled with fear, I would like you to tune into this vision that you love. Then when you *feel* your energy and feelings calm down, you may continue with your day. Do this each time you are distracted by the energy of fear; fear - meaning anything that is not uplifting and happy.

So, you are energy and you are a creator of energy. You may use your power wisely by sending out good, positive energy or you may bring yourself down by sending out denser fear energy. It's all just energy! It's all just your personal reality. How do you want to furnish your space? Do you want density or do you want light? The choice is yours and always has been. Good luck being the *conscious* creator of your personal reality and your own little world!

⚜

*Y*ou are a miracle of divine proportion. You are part of God and you do not know this as a fact. You may as well be the son or daughter of a king. You do not know your heritage, and so you do not *realize* that the king and queen are actually your parents.

How would you respond if you were to become aware

that you come from this royal line? Would you feel better about who you are? Would you like yourself more than you now do? Would you be more gracious and tolerant, or would you become a sort of dictator throwing your weight around? How kind are you when you get to be the one in charge and on top? How loving are you to absolutely everyone?

These are questions to ask yourself once you become *aware* of your power and ability to *create* your own personal reality. Once again, the way you treat others is more than likely how you are treating yourself. If you are kind to them, you are being kind to yourself. If you are mean or unkind to them, you are being mean and unkind to yourself. The energy runs through your body, and your cells, and your brain, and your organs. You treat you the way you treat others when it comes to-the energy of thought.

So, as you continue to wake up and to love yourself, you *will* begin to love others. Do not worry if you have few people who understand you. This is simply a reflection of how *you* do not understand you. Everything clears up once you wake up. Everything becomes clear once you allow the denser energies to rise up out of you. Once you clear some of the confusion and pain and fear that you are holding on to, you will begin to rise up slowly and steadily until you begin to see yourself and others in a whole new way.

For now, I would like you to think of yourself as royalty. You are all royalty and you all deserve the riches of the kingdom. This kingdom is based on energy and energy alone. It has nothing to do with deserving or not deserving. It has to do with existing. If you exist, you are in the family of humanity. If you are part of this family of humanity, you deserve. If you have been judged by others, you still deserve.

If others have been judged by you, they still deserve. This is a win/win situation and this has been taught by your spiritual leaders in the past. Jesus the Christ told you this and Buddha told you this. You are accepted and loved and you deserve the riches of heaven. You may think of heaven as a far-off place in the sky, but I will tell you now that heaven is right here on earth right now.

You may access the realms of heaven, as heaven is simply a dimension that has been described. Heaven is awareness and heaven is acceptance of all that you love. If you are broad in your acceptance, you may find yourself in heaven on earth. You may actually walk around each day feeling that "life is so good; it doesn't get much better than this." If you knew for a fact that you were descended from royalty and the offspring of a king and queen, would you feel like royalty or would you still feel like low man on the totem pole? You create your position in life by how you judge *you* and how you judge *others*. "They do not deserve," you say. Maybe, maybe not. "You do deserve," you say. Maybe and maybe not - you get to decide, and in deciding against them you are sending out a strong energy signal that says, "I vote against this person." And who does this energy run through and affect the most? And who does this energy bounce back to after it has gone out into the ethers? Right - it is you, its sender. Energy will always return to its origins.

So, if you send out the energy signals that "others are good and so deserving." What do you think you will get back? Here is the trick: if you can't think positive thoughts about another person, do not give them a second thought. Focus on the ones you support and do not focus on those you do not support.

❧

*Y*ou will begin to see great changes in the way you view your everyday life. You will no longer look for problems and you will easily discover and accept the solutions that are intuitively given to you. You will begin to work with spirit and you will reconnect with your own soul/spirit inside of you. You will find that as you take on this new way of being guided through your life, you will regain a semblance of trust. You will not only trust life, you will trust your own guidance to bring you through every situation you create.

So, as you regain trust, you will become more connected and less disconnected from your spirit/soul/source. You will become lighter, as you will be adding spirit to your energy simply by opening up to spirit and connecting with spirit. Spirit is light, and light's vibration is quite high and will assist you in moving into the higher, lighter realms. Your connection, or disconnection, with the spirit/soul/source within you can cause you to lose energy or gain energy. Your source is how you exist. When you lose your connection, you literally go dim and lose some of your potential energy vibration.

I am not talking about religion here, nor am I talking about a belief in God. You may exist, and live, and love, and be nurtured without the belief in a deity or God. You simply accept life and believe all is well. So, how does this agree or disagree with all that you have been taught, or trained, or programmed to believe? It is quite simple really. If you believe that you are in good hands being in your life, you are creating a life that hands you good in place of bad. If you believe that you are safe, then you are creating safety for yourself. If you believe that you are well taken care of, then "well taken care of" is what you get. If you believe that you are good, you get good.

So, how do you connect with your spirit or source if you do not believe in God? God is simply a name that originally described energy that could not be understood. God is a name that described magical and miraculous events. If these events are actually caused by your thoughts and *your* beliefs then maybe, just maybe, *you* are God; and maybe, just maybe, *you* are the one you need to reconnect with. Maybe, just maybe, there is a big part of *you* that you are disconnected from. And since this big part of *you* that you are disconnected from is deep within you, we will call this part God, or God force, or soul, or spirit, or light energy.

You may call this higher part of you anything you wish. In the beginning Liane (my pen) would laughingly call me Norman. The name Norman took some of the fear power away from writing for me. So, you may call the part of you, which is your source, anything that you wish. You may believe in God or not. You may believe in the power of love and you will be believing in a higher power.

It's all energy, people…. It's all energy and you may work with and flow with energy, or you may struggle against and fight against and war against energy. Either way, you will return to your source at some point. Some of you expect to see God, or Jesus, or Buddha, but you will all go back to your source, as you are energy and energy always returns to its source.

You are the creator of your world, and you may assist yourself in rising "up" by *allowing* everyone to have their beliefs and by *trusting* that all is well and in divine, good order. The perfection of life has escaped you. You see what you want to see and you focus on what you want to focus on. Give it a rest... come down off your judgment throne and begin to *allow*, and *trust*, and *love,* which is in its essence, unconditional *acceptance.*

⚜

*F*or the most part you do not *believe* that you are God. You do, however, accept the fact that you are energy. This energy that is you is coming from somewhere. It is coming from the source of your being. It is coming from a giant source or force that is unknown to you now. This force that exists all around you is also *in* you. This force is in the air that you breathe and it is in everything that exists.

You may find it difficult to believe that *you* are God; however, you may find it much easier to believe that you are part of this force that is energy. So, if this force runs through you and also surrounds you, wouldn't it make sense that you have an effect on it, and it would also have an effect on you? Wouldn't it make sense that you could *move* in ways that would *affect* this force that you are floating in? Wouldn't it make sense that in the same way you can cause problems for yourself while swimming in water, you may also cause problems for yourself while floating in this force? If you flail about in water you cause great disturbances. If you constantly

135

flail about, you exhaust yourself and splash those around you and possibly begin to sink. If, on the other hand, you can float and flow with the current, you may stay relaxed on the water for some time and really enjoy the ride.

So, if you decide to continue to fight and argue and stir up energy, I wish you to think of yourself as existing in a huge ocean of water. You have the ability to float and flow, and you have the ability to stir things up and cause big waves that will *affect* those who are near you. Please see the benefit in staying calm and not getting all riled-up about every little and big thing that you see. Enjoy the view by focusing on something you like and enjoy, and let all else float by you. Only stop the things you wish to be involved with or attached to. Your energy is magnetic and you will attract to you that which you are. Let go of what you don't want by focusing on what you like and love. Change your focus and you will see a whole new view.

As you continue to focus on what you love, you will become content and happy. Many of you are afraid of being content as you feel that you may become apathetic and uncaring. Contentment is a space that contains a level of peace. Peacefulness is a lack of fighting and struggling. You fear peace because you *believe* that everything will go wrong if you let yourself relax and let your guard down.

You will not have world peace until you can *accept* peace on an individual level. Peace is your goal. Inner peace will reflect out onto your viewing screen of life, and you will begin to focus on and see peace in your outer world. You do not find peace by looking at war. You find peace by looking at peace. Find areas of peace in the same way that your news finds and focuses on areas of war. Peace is not reported in your news and you do not discuss the latest peaceful events at your dinner table. You tend to focus on and discuss the latest fighting and war. Do not talk about it if you do not wish it to be part of your personal reality.

Now I've done it! I have suggested that you not get involved and not take part in the fight. You are all so full of fear that your minds race to the worst-case scenario, and you visualize the worst taking place with some monstrous dictator taking over the world and destroying your world. You are far too imaginative with *your fear*. Please begin to see how your focus is driving you to create greater fear. You have the power and the ability to create! Look at what you are creating for yourself. Please begin to see the benefit in staying calm and focusing on the good....

☙❧

As far as you are concerned, you have always been a light being. There is no time you were ever *not* light. So, how do we get a light vibration into dense matter? We slow it down and dumb it down until it is barely vibrating. You then allow this very slowly vibrating energy to enter matter. Matter is simply light at its lowest vibration, and when you examine matter you find that it is more space than solid.

So we have spirit, or "light being," vibrating as slow as possible, and this "light being" is then able to align with and merge with the denser energy of matter. Once this *light* has merged with or taken on the suit of matter, it is then allowed to enter and leave at will. Often you will hear about, or read about, out of body experiences and this is what is being felt at the moment spirit leaves for a short time.

Now, when spirit leaves, it does not totally leave, or body would shut down completely. Spirit is essence and is not containable. Spirit often does not enjoy being inside the body, especially if the consciousness is constantly abusing the body. If you could put your body under a spirit or "light being" detection microscope, you might see what appears to be soul energy, or spirit energy, all around this body that you are observing. If you look close you will see *light* emanating from each body on earth.

This light is what many call an aura, except an aura does not describe the totality of this *light*. So now we have this light and it appears to be moving in and around the body. It is as though you walk around in a cloud of *light*, and this is true for each individual. Often you dim this light by your behavior and your thoughts. When you feel down, you affect this *light*. When you are up, you affect this *light*. Often you are down and sick and just not happy, and your *light* will reflect all of this. So, let's say you begin to heal and get very happy. Your *light* will literally shine brighter. This is the basics of *light* energy. When you are up we have more light, when you are down, well, you get the idea.

So people; let your *light* shine by staying healthy and happy!

Now, when your spirit decides it is too low in vibration, it may literally guide from outside the body. It takes a certain amount of *light* energy to keep going, but there is always more *light* than is required to simply move the body. The body literally has light energy that merged at birth from the parents, and this light energy is weak but will suffice and sustain life. The majority of *light* enters the body upon birth, or in the womb, or sometimes long after birth. This is known in certain religious traditions where a name is not given to the child until the child is believed to reveal their name.

Most of what you learn regarding the fetus is from science and from folklore. The fetus is the joining of energy from the egg of the female and the sperm of the male. Now, the sperm and the egg are each made up of cells from the parents, and these cells carry energy from these parents. These cells carry either very dense or very light energy depending on the thoughts, beliefs and feelings of these parents. These cells also carry any guilt, judgment, criticism, love, joy and calming energy that are being carried by these parents. Then we have DNA and all scientific awareness or lack of awareness. We also have all the confusion that is currently running through the cells of both parents.

When the "*light* being" enters the fetus or the child after the birth, the "*light* being," or soul, does so with the *intent* of existing and playing in the material plane. Without the use of a body the "*light* being," or spirit, cannot directly affect this plane of matter. So, the *light* entered *you*, and mixed with all that you are, in an effort to experience this material world, and then return later to the God force, or *light* field, that is the totality of All That Is. Why? Because it can! Why go to Disneyland even though you know that it is not real? It's fun to do.

Sometimes you even come to this material plane with an idea or plan. Sometimes you want to meet up with old friends from the past. Sometimes you want to learn to play a musical instrument. Sometimes you want to bring in light awareness on certain subjects such as love and peace. Others want to come to allow other *light* beings to come through their physical body as a way of entering the earth. Still others wish to write beautiful music or paint beautiful landscapes. Some come to play with nature and some come simply to play and act out a role.

All are from the *light* and all return to the *light*. No one gets left out and no one gets left behind. There are billions of people and billions of reasons for a soul/spirit to enter this beautiful fun playground. If you are not having fun in this playground I would suggest that you move to a new location. Focus on another area such as Fantasy Land or Adventure Land. If you tend to be fearful I would suggest you avoid focusing on any Battle Grounds or the House of Horrors. This is meant to be fun, not to frighten the toddlers who believe it to be real.

You have the ability to be many things. You have the power to create your reality differently by using your thoughts differently. The most important *idea* to hold on to is the idea that absolutely everything is energy. If you were to put this idea to good use, you would let go of most of the grievances and hard thoughts that you hold on to.

Once you let go of the harder, heavier thoughts you can begin to focus on the lighter happier thoughts. You will find that the easiest way to raise yourself "up" is by attaching to these lighter thoughts for now. Once you have developed the ability to catch yourself when you start to bring your energy down, you will then become proficient at being the *observer* of your thoughts. As you become proficient as the observer, you will simply watch any negative or dense thoughts as they go by in your mind, and you will focus on only the thoughts you wish to keep. This takes a little practice, but you will become very good at simply observing the energy of your thoughts.

Once you become a good observer, you will come out of any victim role you have been playing. Most often, if you are in a victim role, you have been setting up huge walls of protection. These walls will become unnecessary once you become the *observer*. Your walls of protection, and all of your defensive strategies, were set in place simply because you were not taught that you have the power to behave differently. If you were abused in childhood (which many of you were) you developed protective methods to keep you safe. Some of you developed anger skills as a way of keeping offensive people away, and others developed avoidance skills as a way of leaving offensive people.

Here is the truth about defensive programming: "it is not wrong nor is it bad. It is simply energy that is being used in a specific way." If you are now seeking to move your energy in an upward direction, you will wish to let go of these defensive, programmed techniques. Why? Because you are going to *release* any dense, fearful energy in an effort to lift yourself "up" to the higher vibrating waves of energy. Holding on to the "fear" of others to the extent that you must avoid them on a daily basis is still holding on to *fear*. Holding on to anger, or revenge thoughts, to the extent that you "let them have it with your words" is basically fighting or going into a verbal battle. You are holding yourself *down* when you wish to go "up."

So, no good or bad or right or wrong. It's all just energy moving through you. Energy moves through you every minute of every day and night. Thought energy is alive and moving within the cells of your body. When you block the energy flow *in* you, by holding on to dense fear energy or dense anger energy, you are creating health problems in a very big way. Let go of the *idea* that you must protect yourself in this way. You may simply move away from any threat to you without the need to physically move. I am talking now about your social interactions with others, not about being physically threatened or accosted by another. It is always smart to run like hell in a true dangerous situation. When you are having a conversation in a social setting, it is not necessary to pull out your personal social defenses. Try to *allow* any conversation to take place by *allowing* your feelings to flow by as your thoughts flow through you. Do not react, simply observe. Your social interactions will begin to flow as *you* begin to flow.

Have you heard of someone who is easy-going and easy to be around simply because they are so accepting of everyone? This is a good way to be *if* you are looking to raise your energy "up" a level.

❧

*T*he most important thing for you at this time is self-acceptance and self-love. Acceptance is the ability to *receive* and love is unconditional. So, unconditional reception is what it's all about.

As you learn to accept yourself you will be lifting you "up" and raising your self-esteem. Self-esteem issues cause you to be fearful and to feel undeserving. As you move up to a new level of self-esteem you will no longer *feel* the need to defend yourself nor your beliefs. You will be confident in who you are and you will *feel* accepted and loved. When you feel accepted and loved, you no longer feel objections towards those who disagree with you. This will *allow* you to let go of your need or desire to tell everyone how wrong they are.

Now, we all know (as I have stated clearly in this book) that telling someone off is not bad or wrong in any way whatsoever. The problem becomes one of movement. Do you wish to move your energy in an upward motion or do you wish to move down? It is all simply cause and effect and movement of energy.

So, as you learn to love *you* unconditionally and to accept yourself just as you are, you will begin to *feel* loved and accepted. Do you ever have days when you are in such a good mood because you are so happy? This is how you will feel. You will not be affected so much by what others say and do. You will be so happy with your own personal reality that you will wish to stay where you are which is in a huge wave of joyfulness and love.

So, continue to see the good in being very kind and loving and accepting of your own self, by running the thoughts and ideas and energies of kindness and tolerance and acceptance through the cells of your body. If you *choose* to put everyone else in their place, you will be putting *you* in your place. So, you determine where, or what direction you will go in, by how you *direct* your energy at others. Do you want someone to go to hell? Guess what that does to you? Do you want someone to be put in their place, which you see as down a peg or two? You get to experience that energy firsthand.

Keep your energy "up," by *allowing* everyone to be seen as doing the best they can from where they are. If you have a hard time accepting them, you will have a hard time convincing the cells in your body to accept you. *You* may find that you can understand people better by *realizing* that everyone has had obstacles to overcome, and no one is spared from emotional pain. In the same way that you have dealt with your emotions and feelings and misunderstandings your entire life, so have they. They are you and you are them.

As you go along on your rise "up" to the higher vibrating realities, you will realize how perception is all in the eye of the observer. You *perceive* everything through your pain and past experiences. You may *choose* to begin to see everything through the eyes of kindness. Start with *you.* See yourself through the eyes of kindness, and give yourself a break by running the energy of love, and compassion, and acceptance, and tolerance and gratitude through *you.*

≈ℳ℘

*T*he first time that you begin to *feel* your divinity will be a big deal for you. You have spent your entire life feeling your human side and to actually *feel* that you are

144

divine will be an eye-opening experience.

When you begin to *feel* more than just human, you will begin to act more than just human. When you literally *know* that God is inside of you, you will behave in a new way. You will act as though you are loving and kind without the need to think about being loving. You will begin to feel as though you have a gift right inside of *you,* and you will begin to nurture this gift. You will no longer scold yourself when things go wrong and you will no longer scold others.

You will begin to flow with life in ways you never imagined. You will begin to see life as magical and giving. Once you get to this point in your waking up process, you will be quite happy and content. No matter what is going on around you, you will *know* that "all is well" as you will have "realized your divinity." You will have risen to a level of vibration that literally allows you to *see* how you are all divine and how everything is, and has always been, in divine order. Nothing is wrong, nothing is right; everything is simply co-existing or on its way to co-existing.

This is how nature works and you are part of nature. You are the one who is blooming and opening up to the splendor of life. You are in a position to experience the magic of "*being.*" You are a divine spirit existing inside of material form, and you are learning to express as spirit while in a form. It is as though you entered a rock, and from within the rock you made it dance. You are a soul inside of and surrounded by the energy of life. You are a soul who entered this dimension to create and explore and have fun. You do not come here to "not" experience. You come for this experience. You come to grow and flourish and to experience emotion and energy and matter. You are here! You made it in!

When you begin to feel and to *realize* what a gift it is to be you, you will weep with the joy of it. You will be so happy when you see the big picture. As you continue to wake up you will feel better and better and more at peace. You will let go of the need to protect yourself from everything that you came to experience. You will begin to freely express your joy without the pretense and solemnness of drama. You will let go of any need for acceptance from others, as you will be so happy *knowing* you, that you will have all the acceptance that you require.

As you continue to awaken, you will begin to ask yourself for greater understanding and compassion and kindness. These attributes are the best of you and you will want to always show your best side, your spirit side, your soul. Your soul will literally be shining through you for all to see. You will meet others who are waking up at this time and your individual divinity will join with theirs, and soon you will all be shining as bright as stars. You will begin to see the divine in others and you will begin to assist those who do not yet *feel* divine, by showing them love and kindness.

You will begin to rise to new levels and the rising vibration of love (acceptance) will affect the earth that you live on. Earth will *feel* these higher vibrations and begin to rise in a whole new way. You will be affecting everything and anything by your vibration just as you now do. You will begin to *raise* the level of consciousness instead of putting it down lower. You, my dear sweet child of God, will begin to recognize your divine light and share your divine light by showing it to others. Begin now. Raise *you* "up" now. Start to see how special you are right now today. Begin to *open you up to the light* now, this moment. It starts now, today. Go for it....

❧

*Y*ou will begin to discover new ways to keep yourself from slipping down from the higher vibration realities. Once you learn how to stay "up" you will break the magnetic pull downward.

You were once headed down in an effort to match the vibration of matter. You (spirit you) wanted to experiment or enjoy the journey into matter. As noted previously, you vibrate at such a rapid speed as spirit/light/soul, and so you are required to slow your vibration in order to match that of matter. Had you not slowed down, you would not have been able to access matter and its denseness. So, you slow down to enter matter, and then you continue to lower your light vibration until matter is comfortable enough with you that it begins to enfold your vibration and make you part of it. As you became more matter and less light, you began to dim your light and lose luminosity. You began to dim and now you are reversing this trend. Not only will your light begin to grow as you begin to vibrate faster, your whole life experience will be affected.

As you continue to turn up the light vibration, you will be adjusting the vibration of the matter that has enveloped you (spirit) and melded with you. What you are basically doing is raising matter *with* you and lifting your world "up" as you rise up. This is ascension. This is the light of God raising this world "up." *You*, the light of God - you are returning to a former level of vibration in an effort to express spirit (God) while *in* matter. This is a good thing and is being observed by many in other dimensions.

You are going up after such a long journey down. You required the long journey down to dig your roots in deep. Just as a plant grows its roots down before it ever begins to sprout, you have grown roots and have a good foothold in matter. This allows you to then shoot upward and become more of what you are.

You will find that, as you continue on this upward journey, you will begin to *enjoy* being spirit or light energy. You will enjoy your new role as a light being and you will thrive.

As you raise your vibration, you will be entering the higher vibrating dimensions, or realities. These realities are basically here for your enjoyment. You will begin to access them by aligning your vibration with them. Use your power tool "gratitude" and use love whenever possible. Remember, love is unconditional in nature. Use your joy to give you a boost up to the higher waves of energy, and you will begin to create more or greater joy by doing so.

You have been prepared. You have all the tools that you require right inside of you. You are being guided and you are doing great so far. Do not give up. Keep yourself well and happy by using your thoughts and ideas wisely. You know how energy works now. You have the information you require to raise you up to a whole new dimension, or parallel reality to your old life. You are on your way and you will do well with this.

My pen and I are going to take a little vacation from

writing and will soon be back with more information and insights for you.

Continue on your journey and remember to always look "up" that is the direction you wish to go at this time....

God

Introduction to
The Loving Light Books Series

There are many ways to go within to your core or your heart center. When you reach deep within your own psyche you will enter the core of your being. This is where soul and spirit resides.

For those of you who wish to reconnect with your own God-self I highly suggest that you read and reread the "Loving Light Books" series. This series is designed to draw you "within" to your own God-self and to allow you to peel away the layers that prevent you from becoming the loving, radiant being that you truly are.

This series of books was received by my pen (Liane) over a 10 year span of time and are quite remarkable. You will be led from an earthly way of viewing life to a more God-like way of viewing life. Everything is subjective in this three-dimensional world that you now call home. You, however, are a spiritual being and your life as a human is out of balance since you decided to enter matter. We will feed you information in this series that will allow you to *perceive* your current life in a whole new way.

These books were written for my channel and are most helpful to anyone who wishes to add more love and understanding to their life here on earth. If you are happy with where your life stands now, I do wish you well. If, on the other hand, you would like to learn more about your own spirit essence and how to connect with the part of you that draws love and unconditional light into your life, I highly suggest you begin your journey *within* by reading these helpful books.

I wish you well on your journey to discovering "you"...

God

Loving Light Books

Book 1 - God Spoke through Me to Tell You to Speak to Him
Book 2 & 3 - No One Will Listen to God & You are God
Book 4 - The Sun and Beyond
Book 5 - The Neverending Love of God
Book 6 - The Survival of Love
Book 7 - We All Go Together
Book 8 - God's Imagination
Book 9 - Forever God
Book 10 - See the Light
Book 11 - Your Life as God
Book 12 - God Lives
Book 13 - The Realization of Creation
Book 14 - Illumination
Book 15 - I Touched God
Book 16 - I and God are One
Book 17 - We All Walk Together
Book 18 - Love Conquers All
Book 19 - Come to the Light of Love
Book 20 - The Grace is Ours

Also by Liane Rich

The Book of Love (Includes - For the Love of God)
For the Love of God – An Introduction to God
For the Love of Money – Creating Your Personal Reality
Your Individual Divinity – Existing in Parallel Realities
For the Love of Life on Earth

"Is it theoretically possible to *receive information* from a God process, since the universal God process is inside everything?"
Gary Schwartz, PhD – The G.O.D. Experiments

God's Pen

I first heard the voice of God in 1988. I was sitting in my back yard reading a book when this big booming voice interrupted with, "I am God and I will not come to you by any other name." I felt like the voice was everywhere - inside of me as well as in the sky around me. I was so frightened that I ran in my bedroom to hide.

This was not the first time that I heard voices. I had been communicating with my own spirit guide or soul for about a year. I guess my depth of fear regarding God, and all that he represented to me at the time, was just too much.

I spent two days trying to avoid the voice of God, which was patiently waiting for me to respond. By the second day I was exhausted from lack of sleep and decided to give in and talk with him. This turned out to be the greatest gift and best decision of my life.

In the beginning the voice of God would wake me in the middle of the night and tell me it was time to write. He said I had promised to do this work (I assumed he was talking about the soul/spirit me). I would drag myself up to a sitting position and watch in amazement as my hand flew across the page, while I tried to keep up by reading what was being written.

It was always so much fun to wake up the next morning and grab my notebook to see what God had written during the night. After some time the voice stopped waking me and I became comfortable picking up my pen and writing for God first thing in the morning. I think in the beginning I had to be awakened while still semi-conscious from sleep so I wouldn't object too much to the information that was being channeled through me.

As I grew less and less afraid (and more trusting) of God, he was able to communicate greater information. Some of the information is quit controversial, but I felt it important to just let it be and not censor it. I present the writings in this book to you as they were given to me.

For privacy reasons I am using a pen name. I asked God for a good pen name and he guided me to Liane which (I was told) in Hebrew means "God has answered."

At one point I became a little concerned about my sanity in all this, so I went to a hypnotherapist to find out what I was doing. Under hypnosis I saw this incredibly huge beam of light with a voice coming from within it. It was a giant "loving light" and felt so comforting and kind. It felt like that's where I came from. After that I stopped worrying about my sanity. If this is crazy, I think it's a very good kind of crazy to be....

In loving light, *Liane*

Loving Light Books

Available at:
Loving Light Books - www.lovinglightbooks.com
Amazon - www.amazon.com
Barnes & Noble - www.barnesandnoble.com
Also on Request at Local Bookstores

Made in the USA
Thornton, CO
01/17/23 22:00:29

75b3e5a0-838e-48d7-b70b-9b1107cfc1d8R01